PHYSICAL MAP OF THE
UNITED STATES

Produced by the Cartographic Division
National Geographic Society
GILBERT M. GROSVENOR, PRESIDENT AND CHAIRMAN

NATIONAL GEOGRAPHIC MAGAZINE
WILBUR E. GARRETT, EDITOR

JOHN B. GARVER, JR., CHIEF CARTOGRAPHER
HAROLD E. ABER, JR., ASSOCIATE CHIEF
JOHN F. SHUPE, ASSOCIATE CHIEF

WASHINGTON, D. C., 1987

Lambert Conformal Conic Projection, Standard Parallels 33° and 45°

SCALE 1:5,675,000
1 CENTIMETER = 57 KILOMETERS OR 1 INCH = 90 MILES

KILOMETERS 250
STATUTE MILES 250

PRINCIPAL HAWAIIAN
ISLANDS

AMERICA

AMERICA

Originated and developed by
NEBOJŠA BATO TOMAŠEVIĆ

Text by
STANE STANIČ

Design by
MIODRAG VARTABEDIJAN

Photos by
MIREILLE VAUTIER, ALINE DE NANXE

Many thanks for all the careful planning
& preparation, making our holiday
more than memorable!
Much Love
Mum & Dad
Sept - Oct '95

FLINT RIVER

FLINT RIVER PRESS LTD.
26 Litchfield Street
London WC2H 9NJ

A Motovun Group Book

© Flint River Press Ltd.

First published in
Great Britain in 1989 by
Flint River Press Ltd.
26 Litchfield Street
London WC2H 9NJ

Distributed by:
Philip Wilson Publishers Ltd.
26 Litchfield Street
London WC2H 9NJ

Originated and developed by:
Nebojša Bato Tomašević

Photographed by:
Mireille Vautier and Aline de Nanxe

Additional photographs by:
Tomislav Peternek
The Photographers Library, London
The Daily Telegraph Colour Library, London

Text by:
Stane Stanič

Design by:
Miodrag Vartabedijan

Translated by:
Nada Kronja

Editorial:
Madge Phillips

Production:
John S. Clark

Project co-ordination:
Hugh Merrell

Color separations by:
Delo, Ljubljana
Summerfield Press, Florence

Printed and bound in Yugoslavia by:
Delo, Ljubljana

ISBN 1-871489-00-8

CONTENTS

ceanica Classis

Foreword

Whatever the United States of America and its 240 million Americans do or just look like doing always has ways of reverberating around the rest of the world. Its trade and industry, its policies and alliances, its military moves and domestic disturbances, even the state of health of its leaders, as the stock markets show, can spark off a chain of reactions – pleasant or unpleasant, desirable or undesirable – in places far removed.

Some people stand in awe of the United States for this very reason. Others worry that, as somebody once said, "when the US catches cold the whole world sneezes", and it still takes a week to cure a cold, with or without one of the myriad miracle cures around today. Then again, some people just do not like sneezing.

But what exactly is the United States of America? How does it live and breathe? Where is it going? What are the goals of the nation which has taken shape on the land the Old World discovered almost five centuries ago, and made its grand entrance on the world stage just 200 years ago?

This book is an attempt to describe the USA in words and pictures. It traces its roots and pinpoints the heart of the future commonwealth, the first links in the federation, and the fundamental principles and goals laid down in 1787 and 1788. These principles still serve as an inspiration even today when the fifty united states extend over an area of 3,615,123 square miles.

Compared to the total inhabited area of our planet, excluding the Antarctic, this is not so very much – scarcely six per cent. The United States of America covers only a little more than 40 per cent of the North American continent, and in size is smaller than Europe by about the equivalent of Spain. It is smaller than Europe in population, too: even when the USSR is excluded, the population of the United States is less than half of Europe. As individual countries go, China, India and the Soviet Union are more populous, while the Soviet Union and Canada are larger in area.

The mainland of the United States is roughly rectangular in shape, and stretches about 2,800 miles from east to west and 1,600 miles from north to south. If we line up a map of the mainland so that the Pacific coast coincides with the westernmost part of Ireland, the east coast falls somewhere in the Urals, Florida floats in the Mediterranean, while the US-Canadian border cuts through the Baltic Sea. But besides Hawaii and Alaska this leaves out Puerto Rico, the Virgin Isles, Guam in the Mariana Islands, and several other small Pacific and Caribbean islands under US administration.

The size of the United States of America may be grasped a little more concretely from the following comparisons. In area it is equal to 101

The discovery of the New World was suitably publicized, for those times, through the ingenuity of a handful of adventurers who were also talented artists and engravers. Unfortunately, no picture of Chistopher Columbus' ship "Santa Maria" has been preserved. However, judging from a sketch in one of Columbus' letters, it was similar to the ship depicted in this woodcut from 1493. British Museum, London.

Portugals, exactly 100 Hungaries, 37 times West Germany, 36 times Yugoslavia, 31 times Italy, 28 times Finland, 18 times France, 5 times Mexico, 3 times India, or equal to Australia plus Iran, Brazil plus Pakistan, or 450 Israels! The population of the USA is three times greater than Mexico's, four times greater than Italy's or West Germany's, about five times greater than France's, seven times greater that Spain's, ten times greater than Yugoslavia's...

Historically, population density in the United States has been a very important factor. Demographers estimate that at the beginning of 1981 there were still only 67 persons per square mile compared with 261 per square mile in Europe.

Will this continue to be one of America's great advantages? What changes does the future hold in store? To try to find the answers, we have to delve into the past, into history – go back to the beginning.

Hochelaga, a fortified Indian settlement in the region of present-day Montreal. From a drawing by G. B. Ramusio in Navigationi et Viaggi, *Venice, 1556.*

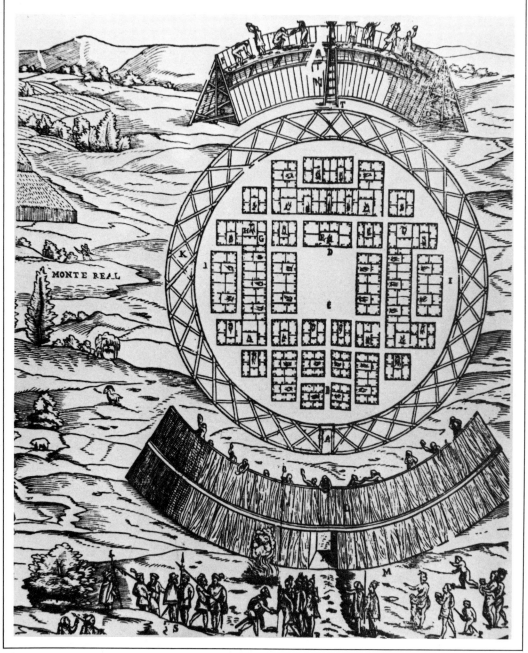

1.   In other parts of the world Americans can usually be picked out quite easily by certain distinguishing features of appearance and manner. But although there is a certain conformity, enough to make them recognizable as a group, many details point to a strong taste for individuality.

2.   American emphasis on individuality has led, perhaps paradoxically, to the proliferation of clubs, associations and groups dedicated to a vast variety of interests, beliefs or causes. The vociferous anti-war groups certainly made their mark: some former US presidents and Pentagon teams remember them all too well.

3.   Non-Europeans are a prominent feature of the United States' demographic scene, and one that is growing in significance. By 1987 there were over thirty million coloreds in the country and their share of the population was rising. The black population, for example, increased twice as fast as the white in the 1980–1984 period.

NO MORE HIROSHIMAS
NO MORE WAR

6

4.   Despite America's growing wealth and sophistication, and the undoubted convenience of streamlined fast-food outlets, there will always be a lot of people ready to indulge in the pleasure of more traditional, homely fare.

5, 6.   For almost a century, the US film industry, the biggest in the world, has been projecting around the globe the landscapes, life and people of America. The first-time visitor to the country finds it hard to shake off the sense of familiarity, the feeling that he has been there before.

7.   Svelte black charm seems to be all the more tantalizing for its element of mystery. It takes only a few simple touches, carried out with innate flair, to enhance the enigma.

8

10

8. Children accustomed from infancy to the extraordinary dazzle of neon signs are not content with anything but bright colors.

10. Tastes acquired at an early age do not change easily, as witnessed by this sheriff, or senior citizen who likes to feel like a sheriff.

9. The street is the source of some of the earliest joys of living, which even grown-ups find hard to resist.
Europeans are struck by the refreshing lack of inhibition displayed in public places.

Last Full Week in July

11.   Quite unexpectedly, which usually makes it all the more enjoyable, a publicity stunt or a parade can start up in the middle of a crowd. As a rule the girls taking part attract attention with more than just their outfits.

13.   When sun-glasses fail to conceal a discreet warm smile, certain other items of a more compelling character become all the more important if you have to enforce regulations.

12. Some coverings make people stand out, especially against a dark background. But it is not always polite to stare, especially when it is time for the midday sandwich, which always tastes better in company, wherever it may be.

14

14.   Anyone can join in the street debates,
as these more or less temperamental
exchanges may be called; they generally
take place in the spirit of the well-known
'American freedoms', with no regard to
sex, color, religion and the like. Which side
wins is usually decided by the age-old
rules. If there is a winner.

15.   As in this everyday scene, barriers restricting freedom may be erected only to protect property rights, safeguard public order, and prevent crime. In 1985 crime in the USA was on the rise after several years of decline. But the Federal Bureau of Investigation was of the view that this increase could not serve 'as a predictor of future statistical trends'.

16

16.   Chilling statistics, such as the 12.4
million crimes, including over 1.1 million
car thefts, committed in 1985, may so
disturb some souls that they take to the
streets to warn of impending divine wrath
and put the fear of God in passers-by.

17.   Two-thirds of the US population
profess a faith, but only a minority proclaim
their religion by their style of dress. There
are about 80 million Protestants, more than
52 million Catholics, about four million
members of eastern Orthodox churches,
and nearly six million Jews in the USA.
Approximately a third of the world's Jews
live in America.

18.   Who knows what the future holds? One thing is certain, more and more young Americans are graduating from college with much pomp and gaiety. But at the same time, the proportion of the population between five and seventeen years is declining. Not long ago a third of all Americans were in this age group; today they make up barely a fifth.

19.   The future certainly looks brighter for the blacks. The seventies and eighties brought them much more self-awareness and confidence.

20. There is a multitude of ways to express patriotic feelings, and just as many different ways to find the courage to face tomorrow.

21. Confrontation with the AIDS threat
has had a strong impact on sexual
relationships. Speedy readjustments
encompassing all age levels and classes
have brought major changes in attitudes
and behaviour.

22. Sharing a harmonious life together
from an early age, with no thought to
differences in sex, race or the like, has
become more common over the past few
decades. The quality of communal life will
also be enhanced by increased concern for
and appreciation of the natural
environment.

23.   Ice-skating in Central Park, a virtually unspoiled area of green and water, enclosed on the east by Fifth Avenue, with its famous luxury apartments. On Central Park South, the Plaza Hotel stands out in contrast to more recent highrise hotel and office buildings. Central Park West (behind) is noted for its Old World-style apartments of the unconventional and cosmopolitan bourgeoisie, many designed by Stanford White, one of America's most original domestic architects of the turn of the century.

24.   It takes so little to fill hearts with a sparkle of optimism even when times are hard and life is fraught with worries.

25.   Which winds carried adventurers from the Old World to the unknown continent, and where and why they dropped anchor – these are a perennial American topic of discussion.

NEW ENGLAND
&
THE SEA

MODEL MAKER

SCRIMSHAW

SHIP MODELS

26–28. The voyages of John Cabot (1497), and Francis Drake (1579), the expeditions of John Smith (1607), who founded the first English settlement, Jamestown, and Henry Hudson (1609), the arrival of the Pilgrim Fathers (1620) – all left an indelible imprint on much of the North American continent. Many of the names they gave to settlements and regions in honor or nostalgic memory of their homelands have been retained to the present day.

29.   The new rises boldly up into the sky
while the patrimony preserves the charm
and spirit of a more human scale.

30.   The spare vertical lines of this
contemporary commercial-residential tower
would have looked cold and barren had the
city fathers not insisted that the traditional
house of God be preserved.

31

31–33. Although the legacy of the Anglo-Saxon founding fathers would scarcely satisfy the comfort standards of even the less prosperous American today, the traditional township with its green lawns, trees and gardens remains part of the American dream, an aspiration of many young couples, regardless of their ancestral homelands.

34.

34. *Transported on the wings of imagination, the multi-colored balloons of dreams, today's generations are conquering new frontiers for the world of tomorrow, just like their predecessors in the past.*

ROOTS

THERE WAS A MIX-UP EARLY IN AMERICAN HISTORY, at about two o'clock in the morning of October 12, 1492. On the sailing-ship *Pinta*, part of a small exploratory Spanish fleet, the night-watchman shattered the still air with the thrilling cries of ''Tierra, tierra''. On the SS *Santa Maria*, the Italian-born fleet commander, Admiral Christopher Columbus (alias Cristobal Colon) tumbled out of his bunk to see for himself. Exactly which coral island in what is now the eastern Bahamas he actually saw — whether Watling, Mayaguana, Samana, Conception or some other — is still hotly disputed by the historians. But whichever it was, Columbus was in the wrong place!

With the patronage of Spain's King Ferdinand and Queen Isabel, he was sailing the seas in quest of a shorter route to China. He had set out westwards from Hierra in the Canary Isles thirty-two days before and, presuming the world to be a much smaller place, even half as big as it really is, he concluded that he had finally reached the eastern fringes of Asia. In triumph he planted the Spanish flag on the island and proclaimed his sovereigns' possession of the new-found land — East India!

Succeeding explorations gradually set matters right. In 1497, John Cabot (the anglicized Giovanni Caboto, another native of Genoa), sponsored by King Henry VII of England, approached the mainland of the continent by way of Newfoundland. Then Columbus himself finally made a landing on the mainland in the south on his third voyage, in 1498. But it was Amerigo Vespucci, another Italian, who first surmised, one year later, that South America was a separate continent both distinct and distant from Asia following his expedition to the mouth of the Amazon. His suppositions gained sway and in 1507 the newly-recognized continents were renamed after him. But final proof was only gathered in 1519–22 when Ferdinand Magellan sailed down the southern coast and discovered the 'southern passage' to the Pacific. Like many an intrepid explorer, he paid for his daring with his life — in 1521 in the Philippines.

Be that as it may, for most people today, including Americans and especially the pale-faced ones, the history of both the Americas and the United States of America began on that October morning in 1492. In a sense that was when the avalanche started moving.

THE FIRST AMERICANS had reached America much earlier, however. Precisely when has not yet been established. Experts reckon that they arrived some time between 25,000 and 50,000 years ago and the very latitude of this time span shows how uncertain the dating is. It is speculated that they migrated from cold Siberia, traveling across a natural land-bridge to Alaska, then climatically more agreeable, and gradually fanning out across the continents. Over the succeeding millennia these first settlers evolved in separate, distinctive groups. But under the influence of geographical factors, and with physical and cultural interaction, various common features began to emerge. When the Old World adventurers landed they found great diversity of ways of life, and in the level of well-being and development, which generally was not as advanced as the European.

The Vikings may have made expeditions across Ireland and Greenland and into North America some five hundred years before Columbus, but no definite traces have yet been found. Viking sagas speak of 'Vinland', 'Markland' and 'Helluland', located by some geographers along the east coast of Canada. Some corroborative finds have been unearthed at L'Anse aux Meadows in northern Newfoundland. A score or so years ago, a medieval map was reported to have been found in a codex from Basel, Switzerland, dating from about 1440. This clearly attributes the Vikings with North American discoveries. On the extreme left of the map of the 'whole world', as it was then conceived, it shows 'Vinland Island', discovered by 'Bjarni Herjolfsson and Leif Eriksson in company', as the explanatory note says. It is hardly likely that Columbus ever saw this map, if indeed it is authentic. But it is quite certain that tales of distant lands and sightings had been circulating among seafarers for centuries by the time ambitious monarchs dispatched enterprising and bold explorers to fill their coffers with gold and claim new territories.

Possibly the Vikings' paths were not retraced for a long time because they did not promise lucrative rewards. Columbus may well have been disconcerted by the first, mostly naked 'Indian' he encountered, who proffered only some skeins of cotton, parrots and hunting darts. To his relief he later noticed that some of the natives had little balls of gold embedded in their noses and heard tell of chiefs further south who had 'great cups of gold'.

Stories of fabulous treasure troves, reinforced by the priceless merchandise trickling across long, perilous overland routes from China, Japan and India, fired imaginations and roused the appetite for conquest and the passion for exploration. Moreover, all that was necessary to establish possession of 'new' lands was to be the first to raise the sovereign flag and proclaim sole rights. The indigenous inhabitants were supposedly granted the vague right to work as much land as they needed to live, but in fact it proved a difficult right to exercise in the face of better equipped and armed conquerors.

THANKS TO THE GREAT EXPLORERS and their cartographic talents, the Old World gradually built up a more accurate picture of the globe. The lust for power, land, gold and other treasures and the driving need for commerce, led the Europeans ever deeper into the American continent. The white man also had much to see and learn from his encounters with the Inca, Maya, Aztec and other civilizations and, despite the tragic outcome for the native population, at least a part of this has been preserved as the legacy of all the inhabitants of the New World.

Tenochtitlan, the Aztec capital, raised on the site of present-day Mexico City, was a splendid sight when the conquistadors first set eyes on it. Outstripping Paris or Rome in population at that time, it stood on a lake with a number of causeways, several miles long, linking it to the shore and to other cities. One of the causeways was wide enough to carry eight lanes of traffic, while two others bore ceramic-lined aqueducts. Similarly breathtaking was the 9,300-mile-long Incan road network which radiated out from the capital at Quito (Ecuador) up into what is today central Chile, boldly leaping rivers and gorges by means of elegant suspension bridges. The fabulous temple-cities, the rites and ceremonials performed there and the Incas' shrewd personnel induction system for captives – all have earned a rightful place in the book of the American heritage. It is a moot point, however, whether there are any historical links between the great American preoccupation with body odors, and the unprecedented Aztec custom of immediately 'deodorizing' foreign delegations with a sweet-smelling incense.

There is a much clearer connection between the dynamic growth of the New World and the indigenous agriculture that had been painstakingly developed down the centuries and produced the all-important corn, potatoes, tobacco, tomatoes, and the like, unknown to the Old World. Farming and preparation techniques were quickly adopted and advanced. But not all. The Incan method of making frozen, dehydrated mashed potatoes, for example, waited a long time for 'rediscovery'.

THE BRONZE-SKINNED, DARK-HAIRED NATIVES were most densely settled in what is today Mexico, where the population numbered between four and five million. The total population of what is now the United States has been estimated at about 900,000, while Canada had only some 200,000 inhabitants at that time. The European colonists adopted Columbus' misnomer and called them all 'Indians', whereas among themselves they were distinguished by tribal names. The tribes differed considerably in stature and facial features, and spoke many different languages. It is estimated that when the conquistadors arrived, some 200 different tongues were in use north of the Rio Grande and around 350 in present-day Mexico.

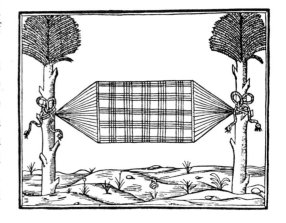

A native hammock, by Oviedo.

Tribes with kindred languages often banded together in more or less stable alliances of nations, such as the Sioux or the Iroquois, a people renowned for aggressiveness and brutality. It was not rare for hostilities to erupt between or even within alliances or nations, leading to the annihilation of one or more tribes. There were wide differences between the tribes in wealth and economic development. While some hunted wild game and gathered fruits, and others were reduced to snaring insects and rodents, Aztecs in Mexico dined on *tortillas* and vanilla-flavored hot chocolate, served in solid gold dishes.

Clashes with the white man who came in pursuit of slaves as well as gold, pearls and precious stones, were inevitable from the dawn of 'modern' American history. While in places the temple-cities were sacked and plundered with alacrity and impatient traders often resorted to the more brutal forms of persuasion in their commerce, generally the Indians were intrigued by the newcomers, often welcoming them as 'white gods', and readily showing them how they farmed and hunted. But soon the white man with his tradition of private property began to fence off the land and the situation rapidly deteriorated. Even in the north, where there was little to plunder, the struggle for survival became a daily affair.

The newcomers were often at odds with each other too, as they vied for the spoils and possession of the land. Rival claims and disputes flared up from the beginning and multiplied steadily, frequently culminating in open attacks and warfare. Spain's first permanent settlement in San Augustin (Florida) was razed to the ground by England's Sir Frances Drake just twenty years after it was founded in 1565. Elizabeth I of England denied the Spanish claim to the territory on the grounds of John Cabot's prior discovery of it.

Enterprising John Cabot had spurred systematic economic activity along the northern stretches of the east coast with his encouraging reports home towards the end of the fifteenth century. English, French, Dutch and Swedish fishermen were soon plying the waters off Newfoundland, seeking the great shoals of fish that supposedly could be hauled out of the sea by the basketful. Catholic Europe had soon gained a new source of supply for its fast-day dinners. Hunters quickly followed the fishermen, with the French trappers proving to be exceptionally proficient and adventurous. One of them, Jacques Cartier, tracked the St Lawrence river as far as the Indian stronghold of Hochelaga, the forerunner of Montreal, and proclaimed 'right of discovery' in the name of his king, Francis I.

The disappointment over Cartier's false gold and diamond strikes, which turned out to be only iron pyrites and quartz, was soon forgotten with his crucial discovery: the route around the Appalachian Mountains and into the interior of the country.

HISTORICAL ACCOUNTS STILL TEND TO BE BIASED in their description of the feats of the settlers, their conflicts and their shifting alliances with each other and the native population. Some historians, for example, extol the English as explorers and colonists. It is a fact that Columbus himself never realized he had discovered a whole new land mass, and it was only in 1522, when the survivors of Magellan's expedition completed the first round-world voyage, that its vastness was first grasped. It is also correct that the English made many important discoveries, especially later on, and even some that others had missed – such as San Francisco Bay, which the Spanish overlooked when they first passed by. Nevertheless, under the prevailing rules of discovery and possession, by far the greatest part of this new world belonged properly to Spain, and the second-largest, eastern Brazil, to Portugal, as was confirmed by Papal decree. But the other Europeans, and the English in particular, undeterred by this, soon began landing on the east coast.

Despite their late start around the middle of the seventeenth century, within 150 years the English had taken the lead in colonization. This is probably why in retrospect the history of the United States is sometimes treated as beginning in 1607, when Captain John Smith laid the foundations of the first British settlement, Jamestown, on the coast of Virginia, which Sir Walter Raleigh had named in honor of the Virgin Queen, Elizabeth.

In December 1620 the *Mayflower* brought the first group of non-conformist Anglican Puritans, the Pilgrims, to Massachusetts. Bad weather forced them to disembark at Cape Cod, where half of them perished in the severe winter. The Pilgrims' stubborn perseverance became a legend. Their code of asceticism, civil organization, solidarity, self-reliance and self-sacrifice, like those of the Quakers and other similar groups, left a deep imprint on the succeeding generations of Americans. The Plymouth Pilgrims originated that great, America-wide feast – Thanksgiving Day – when they celebrated their first harvest, together with the Indians who had taught them to grow corn and tobacco, in 1621. It was the end of starvation and the beginning of plenty.

The Dutch also played a part in exploration and colonization. It was in the service of the Dutch that Henry Hudson, an Englishman, explored the Northwest Passage. In 1609 he opened up the river that now bears his name, traveling from New York harbor all the way to Albany. Dutch fur traders followed his trail within the year and had a post operating in Albany by 1614. Not long after that New Amsterdam was founded, and New Holland began to expand. However, at home the Dutch were more concerned with their burgeoning commerce with Asia and India and their rivalry with Spain on the high seas than with these struggling outposts.

New Sweden started to spring up just south of New Holland, but the Swedes were considered trespassers by the Dutch and were not tolerated for very long. The English saw the Dutch in the same light, and in 1664 a group of just 300 Englishmen, obviously some of the more forceful, succeeded in 'persuading' the Dutch to quit New Amsterdam 'peaceably'. But the Dutch had second thoughts and retook the town nine years later. They held out for only a year before they rechristened it in honor of the Duke of York, and presented it to him as a gift. Instances like these make the inclination to rewrite history quite understandable.

COLONIZATION OF THE NEW WORLD took many different forms, depending on local conditions as well as the circumstances of the mother country. After Columbus' discovery, Spain laid claim to both the American continents, with the exception of Portugal's possession, the eastern part of Brazil. By 1600 Spain ruled over the vast expanse stretching between the Rio

Grande, the Gulf of California and Florida, and extending 5,900 miles southward to Buenos Aires and Santiago. Though Indian tribes retained possession of Argentina and Chile down to the nineteenth century, the conquistadors thoroughly ransacked the great gold and silver treasuries of all the Indian civilizations they encountered.

Around 1700 there was a total of about 32,000 'Spanish' families with some 150,000 members in both the Americas. Travelers reported, however, that there were very few white women, and apparently many of the wives and mothers were Indian. Few as they were in number, the Spanish were the absolute masters of the land while the Indians tilled the soil. Aided by the priests who patiently converted the Indians to Catholicism, the Spanish Crown imposed an absolutist form of government and exploitation based on strict class and racial distinctions. No large number of settlers was needed to man this efficient system, only civil servants, priests and builders – the future cream of the colonies that cherished social discrimination.

But Spain did not only take. Valuable new agricultural products and livestock were introduced in an exchange that on balance was actually in the favor of the Americas. While the New World gave Europe exotic products like potatoes, corn, tomatoes, tobacco, cacao, vanilla and rubber, it gained many more transplants, such as barley, rye, wheat, lentils, rice, flax, alfalfa, apples, cherries, pears, almonds, walnuts, olives, and very significantly, considering the climate there, sugar cane, citrus and tropical fruits, as well as domestic animals.

France did not show much initiative in the early stages of colonization, largely due to its preoccupation with religious wars and social unrest at home. It was mainly left to the fur traders, who proved highly resourceful. These *voyageurs* and *coureurs du bois* spearheaded the French thrust along the rivers and into the interior, following the trails blazed by Jacques Cartier. Their trapping and trading with the Indians led them both north and south of the Great Lakes, and they were the first to master the continent's central waterways. Skirting for the first time the Appalachian Mountains, which had blocked the colonists on the seaboard, they penetrated and opened up new areas. In many respects they adopted Indian ways, often taking native wives and siring many offspring.

But this was not enough to establish a French presence. In the second half of the seventeenth century, for example, there were barely 2,500 roving traders who, moreover, tended to rely on imports to satisfy their needs. Despite their prowess, the able frontiersmen, explorers and administrators were too thinly-spread in their wide domain. Later, the French government began to encourage emigration and colonization, conceived in the spirit of the French feudal traditions that gave estate-owners great powers over their workers. New France finally began to burgeon, particularly around Quebec.

A DISTINCTIVE PATTERN OF COLONIZATION took shape on the east coast of the USA, where waves of settlers began to arrive, driven principally by the difficult economic and social conditions at home, and not uncommonly to escape religious persecution or political oppression. But whatever their individual motives, common to all was the dream of a fresh start, the chance to live a life of their own choosing, according to their own ideals. Few of them had the means to pay for their passage to America. The majority had to rely on private groups of merchants like the Virginia Company of London, the Virginia Company of Plymouth or the Puritan-dominated Massachusetts Bay Company, which equipped, transported and maintained the colonists. In return for this the migrant signed a contract to work as an 'individual servant' for a period usually ranging between five and seven years, on land that the company had been granted by Royal Charter, purchased, or leased from the colonial proprietor.

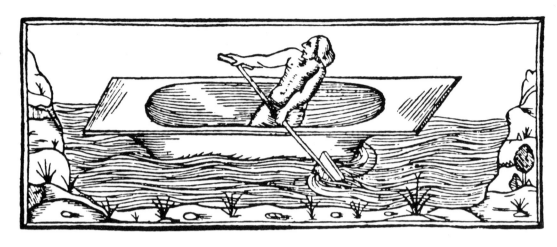

The companies were profit-making enterprises that also engaged in two-way commerce across the ocean. Where Spain's outlays for its overseas conquests were paid off quickly and handsomely by plunder, the process on the east coast was slower and more laborious. 'Investors', skittish as always, sometimes pulled out, leaving the settler to his own limited resources. The immigrant who had journeyed in quest of religious or political freedom in particular took this as a challenge to his dignity and dedication, and redoubled his efforts. To survive and prosper under the harsh conditions, a spirit of community and equality, so much a part of the Protestant ethic, was indispensable. In time this spirit found expression in the pragmatic philosophy which profoundly influenced the way of life of the emerging nation.

A GIANT BRIDGEHEAD FOR THE ASSAULT ON THE CONTINENT was established along the Atlantic seaboard, where a 620-mile-long belt was settled: by the end of the seventeenth century it stretched from Maine to south Carolina. The population rose rapidly as Britain ceased to be the chief source of settlers and immigrants began to flow in from other parts of Europe. In addition to this the birth rate in the colonies was exceptionally high. Children, another set of hands, another shoulder to the wheel, were a major resource in the struggle for a new life. In many settler families the women bore children every second year over a period of twenty to thirty years. Moreover, there were men who married two or even three times.

The flow of immigrants from Europe did not let up. Not even when the British government tried, for the first time ever, to staunch the 'brain drain' as traders and skilled craftsmen began departing in growing numbers. The prisons of the Old World also provided a steady stream of people seeking to erase a stigma that would never be mentioned in America. In the thirteen New England colonies that were eventually established on the Atlantic springboard, in principle and in practice everyone started out as an equal among equals. This in itself was a magnet for many.

At this time, despite the growing thrust and ambitions of the new settlers, the Indian tribes considered nine-tenths of the continent to be theirs. Clashes with the whites had become almost daily occurrences; the more warlike tribes in particular fought constantly, without mercy. But new diseases and the incessant fighting soon decimated the native population, who would not be forced into submission nor enslaved.

The booming colonies looked to Africa for slaves instead. The first shipment was brought in by Dutch traders to Jamestown in 1619. Importation of these 'lifetime' indentured servants, as the slave-traders declared them in their books, soon rose sharply. By about 1700 there were an estimated 20,000 African slaves in the colonies, with more than 3,500 being brought in each year. By the 1780s the black population in the thirteen colonies had already reached 400,000. As the figures themselves show, slavery had become an integral part of the economy, particularly in the more southern colonies and the islands of Central America. In the north, the blacks worked mainly as servants in wealthy households and their life was probably more bearable, although there too the legal code relegated them to a position of profound subjugation and prescribed harsh penalties.

PULSATING WITH UNIMAGINABLE VIGOR, the New World absorbed manpower from whatever source. Besides encouraging immigration, governments and commercial companies did their best to promote the birth rate in the colonies, shipping in women and offering special incentives to men prepared to start a family – like the Quebec administrator who gave away 'an ox, a cow, a hog, a sow, a cock, a hen, two barrels of salted meat, and eleven crowns' to any bachelor ready to take the leap.

Fighting against the native population and gaining one victory after another, in a relatively short span of time the three main colonial powers, Spain, France and Britain, created an entirely new situation on both continents. But the time was clearly drawing near for a decisive reckoning among the powers themselves on the soil of North America. While the Indians still declared themselves the 'true' masters of certain areas, and rising numbers of unwitting slaves were being brought onto the scene, the rival powers tried to out-maneuver one another by military or other means, aligning and realigning as the situation required, according to the shifting balance of forces or relations between their mother countries in the Old World. At the same time, the rapid economic growth of the colonies on the Atlantic coast was fueling the desire for greater autonomy and independence.

In his woodcuts, Hans Staden told the story of his nine months of captivity by cannibals of the Tupinamba tribe (Wahrhaftige Historia und Beschreibung eyner Landtschafft der Wilden, Marburg, 1557).

RUB-MARKS IN THE CASCADE RANGE in the western states of Oregon and Washington are testaments to the precarious exploits of the pioneers of the West. They were worn into the rock face by ropes used to hoist horses and wagons up cliffs and across crevasses in this volcanic massif, in the stubborn search for new fields and havens. It is difficult for the modern traveler, transported effortlessly through rugged mountain ranges and across gorges by snaking highways and leaping bridges, to conjure up all the drama of those first crossings. In the Sierra Madre Mountains, for example, the pioneers had to dismantle their wagons and pass them along the narrow mountain ledges piece by piece.

Today, just two centuries after the founding of the United States of America, no barriers remain. The continent can be crossed 'from sea to shining sea' in about two days in an express train moving at an average speed of 55 mph. A jet plane takes a mere five hours to get from coast to coast, and about three to fly from north to south.

The European immigrants that pioneered the move westward followed natural pathways that had been laid down long before. Scientists consider glacial activity during four lengthy periods in the last million years to have been crucial in shaping the landscape. Pushing down with immense force like monster earthmovers, ice sheets sculpted the relief, excavated and re-excavated the Great Lakes, and scraped great quantities of Canadian soil into the territory of the United States, creating one of the world's biggest and richest agricultural basins.

These upheavels changed the 'natural' courses of two important rivers, the Ohio and the Missouri, turning them back upon themselves and forcing them to find central outlets. It was precisely these 'new' courses that helped the frontiersmen who followed them to open up the interior of the continent.

THE FIRST GLIMPSE OF THE NORTHERN ATLANTIC COAST is intimidating to this day, and its sharp rocks and reefs were fatal for many a newcomer in centuries past. The central and southern seaboard rises more gently out of the sea, making it easier to land and, later, build ports and harbors. This part of the coast corresponds in latitude to the zone of the Mediterranean lying between Lisbon, Naples and Ankara to the north and Marrakesh and Cairo in the south. Southern Florida is only slightly north of, for example, Aswan, Riyadh, Calcutta and Hanoi.

The new arrivals were entranced by their first encounter with the new land. "The air at twelve leagues' distance smelt as sweet as a new-blown garden" records one chronicle from the time of the first settlers. For as far as the eye could see "the vista was of dense woods", and when it was established that these virgin forests stretched almost 1,250 miles inland, it became clear that whoever gained the land would not lack food or fuel, nor materials for building houses, ships or other conveyances.

35. Alaska, the 'last frontier' is the biggest state of the Union. In 1986 it had only about 535,000 inhabitants, but their number is growing apace. Despite the forbidding climate with winter temperatures around minus 40 degrees Centigrade, there has been a net population increase of 132,000 since 1980.

39

36.–37. The 'land of the midnight sun' is a vast expanse of ice. Alaska's rugged mountains include the highest peak on the North American continent, Mount McKinley. Under the icy shrouds, the ground is frozen solid to a depth of some 300 feet, and only the top one or two feet thaw out in summer.

38. Alaska, which means 'great land' in the Aleutian language, is rich in petroleum, coal, copper, gold and other minerals. Its immense natural wealth is a magnet for investment capital from all over the world.

39–41. Fishing is certainly one of the most propulsive branches of the Alaskan economy. Interestingly, concern for conservation is not of recent date: in 1911, the USA, Canada, Russia and Japan drew up a convention on the protection of seals.

42

42–44. The US Government had to recognize Aleutian and Indian land rights and has allocated about a billion dollars for the development of Alaska. This is already having visible effects on the appearance of its virgin landscapes.

43

45. Yellowstone Park, in the northwest corner of Wyoming, was proclaimed a national preserve more than a hundred years ago, in 1872. With its spectacular canyons, geysers and waterfalls, it lies on the high western plateau of the Great Plains, in the foothills of the Rocky Mountains.

48

50

46.   The Frenchmen François France and
Louis Verendrye were the first Europeans
to explore the region of the Yellowstone
River, which gave its name to the national
park that now spreads over 2.2 million
acres and reaches into Montana and Idaho.

47.   Just as in the days when John Calter
was the first Briton to travel through the
area, around 1806, grizzly bear and bison
still roam freely around this extraordinary
landscape. On a calm morning, moose can
be spied taking a bath in the emerald lakes
of Yellowstone Park.

48–50.   About 10,000 geysers, hot springs
and mud volcanoes have been counted in
the Yellowstone National Park. The
bewitched fossil forest and volcanic glass
mountain are outstanding attractions.

Building their new home in New England, the first settlers transplanted the European pattern of rural life. As a rule their houses clustered around a central green where the cattle were put to graze. They staked out their croplands in fields radiating outward from the village. In time the meager soil forced them to turn their energies to other occupations besides farming, but even when they started utilizing the abundant gushing waters for mills and manufacturing, the familiar type of settlement was retained.

Further south, in Virginia, a different pattern of rural life emerged, one that has become so typical of the American lifestyle today. The good soil and favorable climate soon made much sought-after tobacco the chief crop, which entailed an entirely different arrangement of rural living. As tobacco quickly exhausts the soil, the farmers were obliged to move to fresh land every few years. The farm household thus developed into a separate, self-sufficient and mobile unit that had to master many skills and avoid putting down deep roots. The desire to adopt a village type of organization was soon entirely lost. Even when the tobacco farmers reached the foothills of the Appalachians in their constant westward drive and switched instead to grain and livestock farming, they did not relinquish the individualistic 'model' so characteristic of the American countryside.

THE NORTHEAST of the United States is one of seven distinct regions of the country which differ by virtue of their geography, history and economic development. The Northeast includes Maine in the extreme east, Pennsylvania in the center, Western Virginia in the south and Ohio and Michigan in the west.

Three hundred years ago it was a complete wilderness. Today, about two-fifths of the national wealth of the USA is concentrated there. Its ports handle more than half of all the cargoes entering or leaving the country. This relatively small corner of the country holds over fifty cities with a population of more than 100,000. Ten of these cities have more than two million inhabitants, Washington D.C. has over three million, Detroit and Pittsburg more than four million, Chicago over seven million, and New York is approaching the ten-million mark. This massive population concentration, which is linking up the cities of the coastal belt from Boston to Washington into a single vast megapolis and the cities of the Great Lakes area into another, is virtually altering the geography of the Northeast.

Yet the beginning was not exactly promising. The exasperated pioneers had a hard time scraping a living out of the shallow soil, rich only in the rocks and stones left behind by the ancient glaciers. They were compelled to look for a more rewarding means of livelihood, and soon developed several. Nature had been more bountiful to the sea, creating one of the world's greatest fishing-grounds off the Atlantic coast. Small fishing ports mushroomed along the seaboard, soon followed by fish drying and canning plants, whaling stations and whale blubber plants.

The forbidding mountains blocked penetration into the interior for many long years, but the rugged terrain did offer plenty of fast-flowing water, which was soon harnessed to drive gristmills, sawmills, forges and the like, giving an early impetus to the development of manufacturing and industry. Moreover, the water courses and the sea provided cheap transportation for ores, farm produce, manufactured goods and the promotion of commerce in general. Commercial ports began to spring up, spurring on the construction of roads and railways and other transport routes, such as the pivotal Erie Canal. This canal linking Lake Erie to the Hudson River greatly shortened the freight route from the Great Lakes to the Atlantic, and was a major factor in the growth of the Port of New York. The Northeast was soon sending much more freight to Europe than it was receiving. To fill their vessels on the return journey, the shipping companies began to offer low-priced passenger fares

51. Although some 50 or so other national parks have been established since Congress proclaimed Yellowstone the country's first national preserve, its exceptionally impressive scenery and distinctive landforms still make it one of the most famous in the land.

and thus boosted the flow of immigrants. The Port of New York shot ahead of Boston and Philadelphia and began its rise to become one of the most distinctive and populous cities in the world.

On the land the inveterate farmer countered the high yields of more fertile areas by specializing — in livestock farming, especially sheep farming and dairying, and potato growing. To this day, the Northeast is a jumble of farmland and industrial complexes with giant steel mills, glass works, chemical plants, foundries and metal works, rubber plants and machine-tool factories merging with cropfields. Despite the advent of the automobile and aviation industries, which altered not only landscapes but lifestyles as well, the farm sector is still thriving. This devotion to nature is now paying off doubly with the growth of tourism in the wooded hills and mountains, and in the picturesque coastal villages, all within reach of the crowded urban areas.

THE CENTRAL BASIN which rolls away behind the rocky coastal ramparts extends westward for more than 900 miles. Although Americans like to boast that there is 'nothing in the world that can't be found in the USA', it is hard to find anything anywhere else that compares with the vast prairies of central USA. The Basin stretches from Ohio and Indiana in the east, across Illinois and Wisconsin, Minnesota, Iowa and northern Missouri, and fans out into central Texas, Oklahoma, Kansas and the eastern parts of Nebraska, South and North Dakota.

In the northeastern corner of the Basin lie the Great Lakes — huge reservoirs that hold half the world's supply of fresh water. The mighty Mississippi-Missouri-Ohio river system, which gathers water from two-thirds of the United States, meanders about 4,000 miles down the middle of the continent to its outlet in the Gulf of Mexico. The Indians rightly called the Mississippi the 'father of the waters' (or 'great waters' as some linguists say), for with its tributary, the Missouri, it forms one of the longest water courses in the world.

Diligent hands have transformed the prairies, where 'grass stood taller than a man', into the vital Corn Belt, the mainstay of the US economy and a principal source of its prosperity.

At first the pioneers shunned the grassy expanses. Traditionally the European settlers believed that the good soil was to be found under trees, in woods. Laboriously they cleared the virgin forests, hacking trees so great that it took days to saw through them and then battling with stumps so deeply embedded they could not be loosened, and roots so strong they broke plows. Extended by the steady influx of new settlers, the farmlands edged westward, until they reached the end of the forests on the eastern fringe of the basin and crossed the divide into the prairies. The origin of this clear demarcation line is still a mystery. One theory has it that the Indians drew the line by their practice of starting fires to drive game animals into the open.

The thick soil of the prairies was a bane at first. Traditional farm tools and methods did not work in this unfamiliar earth which had been produced by the glacial movements of the Ice Age. The soil was a mixture of powdered rock, deposits from decapitated hill-tops and fresh minerals brought up from the subsoil, which had poured into the valleys to depths of up to 290 feet. Wooden and iron plows were either too light to cut the thick, hard sod, or too heavy to turn the soft, clinging soil beneath. A 'team of six oxen' could scarcely drag the plow. Then in 1833 a breakthrough came when an unknown farmer invented the steel plow by using sections of an old saw. Within a few years John Deere, a farm-tool maker, began to manufacture the hard, smooth steel plows which opened the way to the great farming boom that followed. Another major step was the introduction of hybrid corn, which greatly increased yields per acre in the fields where corn now stands ten to twelve feet high, virtually growing 'before your eyes' — up to two inches in a single night.

Extensive and intricate irrigation and drainage systems played an important part in creating the 'granary of the nation'. The violent, unpredictable Missouri River travels nearly 1,000 miles from the Rocky Mountains to the Mississippi across terrain that may alternately be afflicted by long droughts or sudden devastating floods. The immense Pick-Sloan project to control the river was launched in 1944 and several dams — four of them the largest in the world — have been completed. But the wild, muddy Missouri has not been fully tamed and in many places it is still 'too thin to plow and too thick to drink'.

THE SOUTHEAST is often called the 'changing land'. It encompasses the southeastern corner of the USA — Virginia, Kentucky, south Missouri in the north, and the Carolinas, Tennessee, Arkansas and west Oklahoma in the central area, while eastern Texas, Louisiana, Mississippi, Alabama, Florida and Georgia edge the Gulf of Mexico and the Atlantic. It is blessed by a very agreeable climate, adequate rainfall and a six-month growing season that is free from frost. It is a bounteous land where yields are good and everything abounds, even hydroelectric power, coal, and large reserves of natural gas and precious oil.

In contrast to the Northeast, where the poor, stony soil compelled the settler to turn his energies elsewhere, the Southeast was admirably suited to the farming of products much in demand in the Old World, such as tobacco, rice, indigo, and cotton, which became especially productive with Eli Whitney's invention, near the end of the nineteenth century, of the cotton gin to separate the seed from the cotton. Cotton growing, moreover, lent itself well to slave-labor and the tightly heirarchical colonial system established earlier by the French and Spanish rulers.

But availability of slave-labor was an advantage only so long as the soil was fertile. The low productivity of the unskilled workers was long compensated for by the existence of fresh, rich land, which was relentlesly exploited. At the same time, the ready supply of cheap labor gave little incentive to mechanize farming and raise productivity. But the multiplying numbers of slaves steadily increased the total costs, no matter how much individual costs were kept to a bare minimum. The economy of the Southeast began to falter as new land became scarcer and the tilled soil was depleted. In some areas yields had declined to a quarter of their former level.

The cross-staff, an improved direction-finding instrument, was used by mariners in the early 16th century.

The devastating defeat of the South in the Civil War of 1861–65, in which it lost every fourth adult male and most of its wealth, was compounded by the appearance of the cotton boll-weevil, which destroyed crops from Texas to the Atlantic. Readjustments and change became imperative.

The shift to new crops and methods of farming and diversification of the economy in general proceeded slowly because of the great pools of freed-slave labor available and the unresponsive tenant-farmer system. The instability of world cotton prices added to the problems.

The turnaround only really began in the 1940s. Systematic programs were then inaugurated to put end to the 'combination of poverty and the false economy of low wages' and 'to balance agriculture with industry'. These programs, organized and implemented by local communities, the states, and the federal government, promoted the use of fertilizers, mechanization, the introduction of new crops like peanuts and tree-farming, and the development of processing and manufacturing industries. During the course of the Second World War and in the years that followed, industry, which before had produced only raw materials and semi-finished goods, was restructured toward finished products. The region's rich energy resources — water, coal, oil

and gas – began to be exploited to the full. Mighty oil cities such as Dallas, Houston and San Antonio sprang up.

The Tennessee River Valley project was one of the great public works programs begun in the Depression years. So far thirty-six major dams have been built on the Tennessee and its five principal tributaries to bring its raging, erosive torrents fully under control, to generate electricity and to promote the development of the region. When the project started, this 'pocket of poverty' was ranked as the nation's most pressing problem. Today it looks like a parkland, its water courses transformed into a series of long, clear, navigable lakes which are linked by inland waterways to twenty states. Freight traffic has been increased more than a hundred times over. In 1981, 115,000 million kilowatt-hours of electricity was supplied to homes and industries throughout the central South. Yet this crucial system rests on a network of housewives, farmers, clerks and the like in different parts of the Valley who take a few minutes a day to monitor the local water and rainfall levels so that it can function efficiently.

Major cities of the Southeast include Atlanta, with two million inhabitants, and Houston, the nerve-centre of the US space program and the biggest of the cities with its four million people. Despite the rising beat of its pulse, New Orleans in Louisiana has carefully preserved its aura of old-world charm from the days of New France, while Florida boasts of its space-age launch pads at Cape Canaveral and continues to bask in the glory of its magnificent sandy beaches. It is no surprise, then, that only four percent of the population of the Southeast today works in the once overwhelming agricultural sector. Or that as many as three-quarters of the growing work force are employed in the tertiary sectors – the hotel, catering and service trades, so typical of places with high standards of living.

THE GREAT PLAINS lie west of the invisible line that quite clearly divides the North American continent in two: the 20-inch rainfall line, one of the most important geographical boundaries in the United States. Cutting almost straight down the middle of the country, the line marks off the more hospitable East with its easier farming, more comfortable living conditions and denser population, from the arid West that lies in the rain-shadow of the Rockies, with its unpredictable and low rainfall, harsh climate and smaller, more scattered population.

The 'Great American Desert', as it was long called, covers the area of Montana and North Dakota in the north, South Dakota, Wyoming, Nebraska, Colorado and Kansas in the center, and New Mexico and western Texas in the south. This 400-mile-wide wedge tilts upward gently toward the Rockies in the west. It has a marked 'continental' climate with scorching summers and icy winters. The 'Great Blizzard' of a century ago (1887) buried people, buildings and millions of cattle under snow drifts 100 feet deep. But years may pass by with scarcely a drop of rain in this climatically capricious land.

The climate and the hard, dry earth long deterred settlers. Roving hunters and trappers, carrying only the bare essentials and with an animal or two, braved the treeless desert for short spells. Only the Indians were able to live there on a more or less permanent basis. Riding horses that are supposed to have bred wild from the stock first imported by the Spanish, they hunted the teeming buffalo, which supplied almost their every need: meat and milk, hide for clothes or tepees, and bone for tools and weapons. But the tranquility of the wilds was shattered in 1868 when the railroads reached the Great Plains, bringing well-armed commercial hunters. The great herds of buffalo were rapidly annihilated and the Indians were forced into retreat.

The fabled cowboy and his milling herds of cattle took their place. The prevailing theory has it that the Great Plains became America's cattle country as a result of a few strays that escaped from Mexico centuries before. In the

*Conversation with an uncomely Indian woman, by Girolamo Benzoni (*Historia del Mondo Nuovo, *1565).*

space of something over 200 years, the six cows and one bull imported by the Spanish into Mexico in 1521 had produced an estimated five-million-strong herd of cattle in the Great Plains. It needed only a good horseman with a lasso and the strength to endure cattle drives of several hundred miles to the railheads further east, to get the cattle industry under way. Of course, it also took the stamina to withstand Indian attacks, the violent climate with its fierce storms, flooded river crossings and bone-dry tracts of desert. The Great Plains provided all the stuff of the great tales of the Old West. The East gave the meat-packing plants, the market and the motive.

Would-be settlers continued to pass through the region as long as there was better land to be had. But once the fertile valleys of the Pacific seaboard were occupied and there was little free land left in the East, the Great Plains attracted more interest. Homesteaders began to take up the government grants of 154 acres and join battle with the land and the elements. Immigrants from northern Europe, more accustomed to such hard conditions, tended to make up the bulk of those who survived. With them, they brought the seeds of the all-important winter wheat. Today, giant combines start reaping the golden grain at the southern edge of the Great Plain each spring and travel in a great arc northward right up to the Canadian border, harvesting the vast expanse of the US winter wheat belt.

But first the homesteaders had to come to terms with the Indians and the even more hostile cattlemen. The strife between the 'sod-busters' and the ranchers – the farmer and the cowman – has been recorded for later generations by the tales and the ballads of the cowboy. The singing cowboy was no figment of the imagination of Hollywood movie moguls. Afer a hard day's drive it was essential for the cowboys to calm the cattle with their lilting songs and, above all, to keep them from stampeding – one of the greatest dangers on the trail. The cowboy and his sentimental ballads have become part of American culture, and the core of the Great American Legend.

Natural disasters, like the Great Blizzard, which is credited with breaking the ranchers' power and forging a compromise with the homesteaders, have helped to shape the rugged individuals of this region, with their strong tradition of cooperative associations. In time, industry and oilfields have also added their own stamp. Flourishing cities like Denver and Colorado in the foothills of the Rocky Mountains show what can be built out of nothing, and why.

THE MOUNTAINS AND DESERTS, as geographical terms, primarily refer to the Rocky Mountain range, running almost vertically from the Arctic to Mexico like a giant backbone of the continent, and to the lands lying west of the range and of the Rio Grande to the south. The West Coast valleys below the Cascade and Sierra Madre Mountains are not included. The region covers parts of Montana, Wyoming, Colorado, New Mexico and Texas in the east; Idaho, Utah, Nevada and Arizona in the middle, and sections of Washington State, Oregon and California in the west.

While the rest of the country is interlaced with a rich network of water courses, the land between the Rocky Mountains and the Sierra Nevada in the west is dry; the sun beats down for nine-tenths of the year, the thermometer can climb to over 50 Centigrade in the shade, and even fairly large rivers from the mountains die before they can find a way out of the desert. But it may rain occasionally, as in midsummer, and then the desert blooms in a blaze of color. But with so little plant cover the desert shifts constantly, while the mountains around it are steadily eroded and reshaped into strange forms.

In short, this is an area the pioneers left just as quickly as possible on their march West. It was only in 1848, when John Augustus Sutter, a German-born immigrant, discovered grains of gold in a mountain stream in California, that the situation changed dramatically. Gold Fever erupted, bringing a rush of hopeful prospectors and miners. The Mother Lode that Sutter had helped locate was exhausted in only ten years, even though it was some 120 miles long and a mile wide. But the Fever did not abate; the prospectors spread into the Rocky Mountains in the frenzied hope of striking it rich. In the latter part of the last century rich deposits of tin were discovered in South Dakota, and silver, lead and copper in Montana, areas that are still powerful mining-metalurgical centers. The largest open-cast copper mine today is located at Bingham in Utah. On the slopes of the Great Salt Lake, which contains 6,000 million tons of salt, or another lake with millions of tons of soda, giant excavators fill interminable lines of rail cars with these minerals. But many of the 'strikes' were short-lived. There are numerous ghost-towns in the region, like Tombstone and Cripple Creek, that stand as monuments to human folly and the voracious exploitation of the earth's riches.

Death Valley, the 'bottom of the USA', lies buried in this part of the country, where the earth has been violently folded, compressed, heaved up and crushed down for 100 million years to form some 40 mountain massifs and numerous Pacific islands – in fact, submerged mountain tops. An ancient lake-bed, now a desert, more than 125 miles long, Death Valley is 276 feet below sea level. Lying in the Rocky Mountains, too, is the continental divide: the point from which, theoretically, a ball if thrown to the east would roll eventually to the Atlantic, and if to the west, into the Pacific Ocean. The Colorado River, for example, which cuts deep into the desert floor creating one of the world's wonders, the Grand Canyon, flows into the Pacific, while the Rio Grande which rises close to the Colorado, but on the other side of the divide, waters the whole of the south-west on its 1,885-mile journey to the Gulf of Mexico. Then again, in the extreme northwest corner of the USA, the Columbia River, much shorter but still one of the six longest rivers in the country, flows into the Pacific.

Construction of the Grand Coulee Dam, the largest concrete dam in the USA, which forms the Lake Roosevelt reservoir on the Columbia River, has turned nearly one million acres of arid wilderness into farmland. This and other projects have tamed the Columbia completely, whereas some stretches of the Colorado are still unregulated and destructive. The 650-feet-high Hoover Dam brings one part under control in a system which supplies electricity to Southern Californian cities and industries and irrigation waters to hundreds of thousands of acres of thirsty soil. Long ago the Indians used the waters of the Rio Grande for small-scale irrigation. Their 'know-how' is being applied wholesale today to water the immense, flourishing fruit-growing industry which has become one of the leading branches of the economy in this 'desert land'.

Los Angeles, Hollywood and Silicon Valley, with its 'information era' electronics research laboratories and sophisticated plants, are clustered together in a rather narrow section south of Death Valley and the Sierra Nevada. But rigs pumping the 'black gold', oil, still seem to be the main source of prosperity here, as in other parts of this geographical region. Eight railway lines and a dozen highways crisscross this once inaccessible part of the USA which has firmly taken the lead in many domains; not least of all with its 'fantasy' industry, including Disneyland and the much more down-to-earth but equally imaginative nature preservation projects. The Yellowstone National Park was established as the nation's first nature reserve in 1872. Its 3,500 square miles of wilderness contain the world's greatest geyser area, numerous waterfalls and deep canyons. Several of the nearly 50 national parks formed around the country since then are also located in this region: the Mesa Verde Park with its prehistoric cliff-dwellings, the Rocky Mountain Park, Yosemite, and the Grand Canyon National Park.

THE WEST COAST VALLEYS, the smallest of the geographical regions of the United States, form a 100–150-mile-wide belt that runs some 1,250 miles southward along the Pacific coast from the Canadian border almost to Death Valley. Lying to the west of the Sierra Nevada and Cascade Mountains, it encompasses the three westernmost states of the Union: Washington, Oregon and California.

For a long time the lush West Coast was an unattainable dream for easterners. Reaching the Pacific coast from Boston or New York entailed many months of sailing, first down the east coast of the Americas, around Cape Horn and then northward. But on the shores of the Pacific, at Puget Sound, sculpted by glaciers thousands of years before, along the Columbia River and its tributaries, or in the Sacramento and San Joaquin valleys, there was great natural wealth waiting to be tapped. Travelers returning from these parts brought tantalizing stories of an earthly paradise with a gentle climate, rich pastures, and gigantic trees that must have been saplings 'when Christ was born'.

The first caravan of pioneers reached this new Eden overland in 1826. The hard-bitten hunter who led it from Independence on the Missouri River chose a route through the South Pass, which was the only gap in the Rocky Mountains caravans could negotiate. The journey took four months. It was so daunting that some 17 years passed before migrations began in earnest. In 1843, 1,000 daring settlers started out on the great trek from the Mississippi Valley, the following year 1,400, and the next another 3,000 decided to try their luck. Their pioneering spirit became a legend and a great inspiration that has been immortalized on film.

Many of the first settlers to venture across the continent came to rest in the valleys between the Cascade and Sierra Nevada Mountains and the gentler coastal ranges. But the majority pressed on, below the Klamath Mountains, to the 500-mile-long Great Central Valley, drained by the Sacramento and San Joaquin Rivers before they empty into San Francisco Bay. This is one of the most productive farming regions in the USA.

Everything thrives here: vegetables of all kinds, grown by the most up-to-date methods, are harvested all year round. The black soil of the delta nourishes the 'green gold valley', where lettuce, beans, rice and onions flourish, along with a wide variety of fruit, from peaches and apricots to almonds, avocados, olives, oranges and grapefruit. The sunny climate with sufficient rain, trapped by the high mountain ranges, is well-suited to grain, cotton and vinegrowing. Livestock farming has also developed strongly in the midst of all this abundance. Streams of trains and trucks laden with fresh produce set off for all parts of the continent each day.

But this is all of rather recent date. Fifty years ago the area was hardly able to feed itself because of the poor rainfall pattern. In the Great Central Valley, water was abundant at the wrong time. While winter floods presented a serious problem, the summers were dry. Moreover, most of the available water was concentrated in certain areas of the Valley, with some parts, like Williamette Valley to the north, getting far too much and others far too little. The resourceful settlers decided to improve on nature. They built numerous dams and canals to distribute the water to the right place at the right time, and in the right quantities, and in the process created the evergreen, ever-flowering garden of today.

Puget Sound, a narrow inlet of crystal-clear, blue-green water, is situated at the northwestern tip of the United States amid misshapen, snow-capped mountains, formerly volcanoes. The erstwhile fishing villages dotted along this natural harbor – Seattle, Portland, Everett, Tacoma, Bellingham and Olympia – were among America's first windows on Asia, just as the New England ports were its openings to Europe. The mountain slopes south of the

5

Sound are covered by giant Douglas firs and other conifers unknown in the rest of the world. Below them, particularly near the mouth of the Columbia River, lie the great salmon fisheries. After two to seven years in the sea the salmon return there on their way to their spawning-grounds in the inland streams or lakes. The salmon's strange life cycle has led the pragmatic fishermen to study it carefully in order to protect it. A great deal has been done already to ensure a sufficient supply of salmon: artificial hatcheries and special 'fish ladders' running up dams and rapids have been constructed.

Similarly, great efforts have been made to protect and renew the precious forests of the northwest. At first they were ruthlessly felled with no thought to the harm being done to the delicate ecological balance of these natural 'communities'. Timber resources, the animal life in the forests and the soil itself had already been damaged over wide areas when the US Department of Agriculture set up its Forest Service in 1905, and initiated serious research and control of forest management and the forest-related industries.

THE FORTY-NINTH STATE, ALASKA, joined the Union only in January 1959, although the United States had purchased it from Russia in 1867 for $7,200,000, or less than two cents an acre. The biggest of all the states, it has the smallest population: around 500,000 people.

'The land of the midnight sun', 'the last frontier' or translated from its Aleut name, 'the great lands', Alaska is truly an immense territory. But it is a land of ice. Under the icy shrouds the soil is frozen solid to a depth of 290 feet, and even in summertime, when the sun never sets, only the top two feet thaw out.

At first glance, the realm of the polar bear still looks much like 'Seward's icebox', as it was derisively dubbed immediately after Secretary of State William H. Seward arranged the historic purchase. Because of its inhospitable conditions, it took quite some time for Seward's 'folly' to be properly appreciated. The climate is harsh in the extreme. In the far north the temperature drops as low as −40 degrees Centigrade, and snowfalls can be up to 36 feet deep. The winters are a little more bearable down south, but summer there can be unpleasant. In the capital, Juneau, which lies close to

Hunting with the aid of snowshoes in the northern winter, from a drawing by A. Thevet (Singularitez de la France Antarctique, *1558).*

52. *The epitome of the 20th-century city, New York constantly fascinates anew with its architectural 'sculptures' of such gigantic scale that they might conceivably be observed by intelligent beings on some distant planet – if any exist and have nothing better to do. Can New York really be decaying?*

53

53–54. *New York State boasts the epithet 'the Empire State' and a population of 18 million people living in an area of only 48,000 square miles. Notwithstanding Buffalo, Albany, Syracuse, the Great Lakes, Niagara Falls and other places of interest, the State's greatest drawing card is New York City, with more than seven million inhabitants, on just 300 square miles. The 'core' of the Big Apple is Manhattan, an asphalt, glass and cement jungle with 24,000 people squeezed into each square mile.*

56

55–56. *New Yorkers unquestionably appreciate the two airports they have at their disposal, as well as the four heliports, two railway terminals, forty bus carriers, the extensive subway network, excellent ferry system and four underwater tunnels. But they take more pleasure in the square mile of green lawns and parks downtown. Inured to crowds, nothing disturbs their repose amidst 100,000 or more other people – as long as it doesn't rain!*

57

57.   This city of myriad amusements and entertainments has a reputation as one of the most dehumanized agglomerations in the world. Of late, new ways are being found to pretty-up and revitalize the decaying inner city areas.

58.   Many aspiring artists try to breathe soul into this human warren. Sometimes these projects call for considerable sums of money just for paint and materials, let alone the amateur artist's time.

59

59. Each of New York's many bridges has been given a distinctive character by its designer. Although it may be faster to travel to Manhattan by underwater tunnel, thanks to large-capacity access roads, it is hard to resist the pleasure of crossing one of the bridges and experiencing the maestoso of the steel harp's music.

60. New York, Boston, Philadelphia and Baltimore are the principal ports and industrial centers on the East Coast, although New York is way ahead of the rest. The race for primacy was decided long ago, in 1825, when the Erie Canal was constructed and freight costs from New York to Lake Erie were cut to a tenth. When traffic on the Great Lakes was linked up to traffic on the Mississippi, the resulting navigation system ran from the Atlantic to the western tributaries of the Mississippi. The construction of the railway later reduced the importance of river and canal transportation, but by then New York was

already interconnected with the hinterland in several ways.
New York lured shipping lines to its port with its inland connections and low freight costs, becoming America's biggest export harbor. As exports began to outstrip imports, shipping agents started promoting low passenger fares from Europe, to fill the holds on the return journey. Soon New York was the number-one port of immigration.

6

61–63.   Ever since the biggest and best-known 'matchbox' in the world, the United Nations building, was raised on East River, immense façades of glass have proliferated, reflecting the changing shapes and shades of one of the oldest cities in the United States.

Though New York harbor was discovered in 1524 by Giovanni de Verrazano, the river takes its name from the English navigator Henry Hudson, who sailed up it as far as present-day Albany in 1609. His expedition was financed by the Dutch, who laid the foundations of Manhattan in 1626. In 1664 the British took over the site, and New Amsterdam became New York.

64–65. Although the immigrants arriving in New York were mainly from Europe, it did not take long for Chinese from the other side of the globe to discover this great port. New York's Chinatown is famous for its size and exotic bustle.

66. The easiest method to find one's way through the New York maze is to call on the assistance of one of the army of taxi-drivers of every color, race and ethnic origin – there for the choosing. As far as the fare is concerned, a cut price can sometimes be negotiated for a long ride – by those who know how.

66

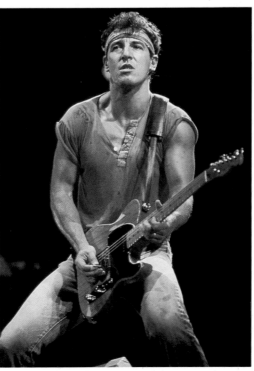

67. The music of black Americans with its pulsing rhythms and infinite improvisations is one of the mainsprings of 20th-centrury music all over the globe.

68–69. American musical theater, especially ballet, has been deeply influenced by jazz. The latest rock styles likewise have their roots in black rhythms and blues. Many white composers and performers, Bruce Springsteen for one, owe much to this source of inspiration.

69

70

72

70–72. *Irrespective of the impact of their culture, blacks remain socially disadvantaged as a group, along with Hispanics from Central and Latin America.*

73–75. New York is still one of the main incubators of new Americans. More than a fifth of its residents were born outside the USA. Just over a third of these came from Northern, Central and South America, a little more from Europe, and slightly over one-eighth from Asia. Today, the inflow of 'fresh' Americans has dwindled to a trickle.

76–77. *The social and economic status of the black population assures a ready pool of applicants for lowly-paid jobs requiring no special qualifications. Most of the top jobs, especially in the world of finance, centered on Wall Street, are still held by whites. Following the civil rights campaigns and revolts of the sixties and seventies, the position of the blacks has generally improved.*

the Canadian border, the Japan Current blowing in from the Pacific can jolt the temperature up to 30 degrees Centigrade and brings incessant rain – as much as six feet annually.

Vitue Bering, a Dane sailing for the Russian Tsar, discovered Alaska, in the colonial sense of the word, in 1747. The very first pioneers, however, probably came from Siberia and Asia, crossing over by means of the stepping-stone Aleutian Islands when they still formed part of a land bridge linked to the Alaskan Peninsula. The 80,000 Eskimos, Aleuts and Indians native to Alaska today are believed to be their descendants. In the most generous land settlement ever made in US history, they were granted nearly $ 1,000 million and 45 million acres of land in compensation for mining and transportation rights in the seventies. For Seward's snowy white elephant turned out to be an arctic eldorado, rich in oil, gas, coal, copper, gold and other metals and minerals. The Prudhoe Bay oil and gas reservoir on the Arctic Coast is twice as large as any other oilfield in North America. The fisheries have been another rewarding resource and one of the most productive branches of the economy.

Seal-fur hunting is still thriving. The seal population has almost been restored as a result of an international treaty signed in 1911 by Canada, Japan, Russia and the United States to restrict and control the industry.

Tourism has even begun to develop despite the natural barriers. A network of airfields is opening up Alaska's principal attractions – national parks, forests and wilderness reserves, particularly in the central section around Mt McKinley which, at 20,320 feet, is the highest peak in all of North America. The gold rushes at the turn of the last century petered out rather quickly, but Alaska is nevertheless blossoming – even without trees.

THE FIFTIETH STATE, HAWAII, became the youngest state of the Union in August 1959. It had been linked to the USA politically since 1900 when, according to official records, the Hawaiians voluntarily requested American citizenship, and their former kingdom became an organized territory.

In 1984 there were just over a million people living in Hawaii. It is estimated that a third of them are descendants of the first Polynesians who came in their outrigger canoes to this wondrous chain of islands some 1,400 years ago. The rest of the Hawaiians are of Euro-Asian origin. Captain James Cook was the first European to discover the cluster of islands some ten years before he landed in Australia.

The eight large and one hundred or so small islands are scattered over an area of 1,600 miles in the Pacific. The island nearest to the Pacific coast of the United States is about 2,000 miles away from San Francisco. Although the islands are not well-endowed with mineral resources, they yield lush harvests of sugar cane, bananas, coffee and other fruits and vegetables. In recent years, industries have been multiplying, attracted in part by the very agreeable climate. Although Hawaii lies in the tropics, the ocean currents and the northeasterly winds hold the mean temperature fairly close to 24 degrees Centigrade all year round.

The third-largest and best-known of these islands, with their breathtaking scenery and quite distinctive character, is Oahu, the site of the capital, Honolulu, and the home of almost half the population. Pearl Harbor, a few miles away, is the base of the US Pacific Fleet. The Japanese attack on this naval base in December 1941 brought the United States into the Second World War. Each year thousands of ships dock in Honolulu's harbor bringing nearly 3 million tourists to bask on the magnificent beaches of this 'earthly paradise'.

The biggest of the islands, Hawaii, twice the size of all the others put together, concentrates in one place all the attractions of the archipelago. Five

78.   Today, New York is just one part of a 50-million-strong megapolis, an almost unbroken urban complex extending 600 miles along the northeastern seaboard from Boston, through New York, Philadelphia and Baltimore to Washington. This is 'Boswash', which encompasses parts of 11 states. But New York will always be New York.

volcanoes, of which two, Kilauea and Mauna Loa, are still active, give Hawaii its distinctive shape. Mauna Loa, the largest active volcano in the world, rises to a height of 13,675 feet, dominating the extensive National Park below and the island as a whole.

THE SELF-GOVERNING, NON-SELF-GOVERNING AND TRUST TERRITORIES of the United States of America include a number of islands in the Caribbean Sea and several thousand scattered across the Pacific Ocean. The most important is Puerto Rico, a rectangular island covering 3,423 square miles in the northeastern corner of the Caribbean. Discovered by Columbus on his second voyage in 1493, it was ceded to the United States after the Spanish-American War and voluntarily opted for association with the United States in 1952. Its population of about 3.5 million people enjoys one of the highest standards of living in Latin America, although the steady stream of Puerto Ricans leaving to take unskilled jobs in mainland American cities probably helps to keep it so.

Guam, the largest of the Mariana Islands, achieved self-governing status under United States trusteeship in 1950. Historically it has been tied to the US since the end of the last century, when it was acquired from Spain. Like many Pacific islands, it was occupied by Japan during the Second World War. US military installations on the island and its budding tourist industry are important for its economy. Guam has been represented in the United States Congress since 1972.

In addition to the other Mariana Islands, American Samoa, some 2,500 miles south of Hawaii, is gradually acquiring self-governing status. In 1981 its 40,000 inhabitants sent their first delegate to the US House of Representatives but, because it is not constitutionally a part of the United States, the delegate does not have voting rights.

Baker, Howland and Jarvis Islands, which are uninhabited, as well as Canton and Enderbury Islands, the Johnston Atoll, Midway Islands, Wake Island and Kingman Reef, are similarly non-self-governing territories of the United States. To visit many of them special permission must be obtained – from the United States Navy Command, for example, in the case of the Midway Islands. The US Virgin Islands were also discovered by Columbus and acquired from Spain. In view of their non-self-governing status, their 100,000 inhabitants hold American citizenship but not all civil rights, such as voting in presidential elections and representation in Congress.

Only a few of the 2,000 islands and islets that comprise the Trust Territory of the Pacific Islands, or Micronesia, are inhabited. The total population of Micronesia is estimated at about 130,000. Besides the Mariana Islands, some of which rise over 3,000 feet out of the Pacific, there are also the Marshall Islands, and the Bikini and Enewetak atolls, the scenes of atomic bomb tests after the Second World War. Prior to the tests some 450 residents were evacuated, but only 55 had returned 30 years later.

All of these territories represent potential additions to the fifty stars on the American flag, which, apart from anything else, could present ticklish design problems.

THE EMERGENT STATE

DIVERSITY IN UNITY AND UNITY IN DIVERSITY is the over-riding impression gained from a quick tour of the length and breadth of this land of continental proportions. This characteristic feature had begun to appear within a century-and-a-half of the foundation of the first permanent English settlement, Jamestown. The colonists' bridgehead on the mountain-trapped Atlantic seaboard had by then been expanded and consolidated to a great extent, welding diverse groups together into a single economic and cultural entity.

The directions and dynamic features of the colonies' development were largely shaped by the fact that the emigrants were plunged into an entirely new life, in which personal resourcefulness and tenacity were the keys to success. The divisions and the mores of the Old World faded rapidly; religious precepts were adapted to day-to-day social and political pragmatism. Only the hardworking winner was blessed by God.

The general development was greatly aided and abetted by what J. Hector St John Crevecoeur, a French scientist and later Consul in New York, described as the 'melting pot'. Referring in his essay *What is an American?* to "that strange mixture of blood which you find in no other country . . . in which members of all the nations of the world are blended together into a new human race . . .", he goes on to explain: "I could point out to you a family whose grandfather was an Englishman, whose wife was Dutch; whose son married a Frenchwoman, and whose present four sons have now four wives of different nations. He is an American who, leaving behind him all his ancient prejudices and manners, receives new ones from the new mode of life he has embraced . . ."

The population grew at an astonishing rate. There were about 250,000 pioneers in the whole territory of North America at the beginning of the eighteenth century. By the second, historically much more crucial part of that century, the number of people 'making history' had swollen to 1.5 million.

In those years, warring with the Indians was an everyday occurrence. But among the colonists themselves the most vital group, the English (or British) and the anglicized Europeans, who had set down such firm roots in New England, were spoiling for a final reckoning with the French and the Spanish.

In the middle of the century, Spain controlled and considered its own an incomparably greater territory than England, particularly when the area around Hudson Bay in present-day Canada is discounted. France held settlements in the valley of the St Lawrence River and in the region of New Orleans, and was strengthening its hold on the whole valley of the Mississippi and its tributaries, such as the Ohio River. The erection of the French stronghold, Fort Duquesne, on the site of today's Pittsburg, was cause enough for fighting to break out between the French and the British of Virginia and

Pennsylvania, who were eager to penetrate into the inviting valleys behind the Appalachian and Allegheny Mountains.

A young lieutenant colonel, twenty-two-year-old George Washington, headed a detachment of Virginia militiamen which fired the opening shots of the 'French and Indian Wars' in 1754. The fortunes of war lay with the British: One by one the French lost their strongholds; Quebec and Montreal fell by 1760. The French had nowhere left to turn and a treaty was concluded in Paris in 1763, ceding all French territories east of the Mississippi to Britain, and those west of the river to Spain.

BRITISH HEADACHES with its colonial possessions only really started at this juncture. The overseas territories in North America had abruptly doubled in size, greatly increasing the burden of colonial administration, which in fact had been rather neglected. Furthermore, greater attention had to be paid to their defense, to reconciling the conflicting interests of the different peoples, the old and the newly-acquired territories, and, not least of all, to ways of financing the imperial administration.

The unprecedented admixture of Catholic French colonists, a large number of partly Christianized Indians, Protestant English and various anglicized settlers further complicated matters. The Old World style of administration had not been particularly well-suited to circumstances in the colonies before, and became less and less so as time went on. Instead of entertaining any notion of sweeping reform, the British attempted to defuse the situation by reserving all the western territories between the Alleghenies, Quebec, the Mississippi and the Floridas for the Indians – by royal proclamation no less. Furthermore, they resolved not to disturb the French in the Ohio Valley. Needless to say, none of this was to the liking of the New Englanders: these vigorous colonists were cramped on the Atlantic seaboard and British policy was effectively cutting off their westward expansion. Ultimately they simply paid little heed to these frustrating proclamations, or to the King and government standing in the way of what they considered their fundamental right to settle new land.

The situation deteriorated steadily over the following years. The Crown administration, in the way of all governments, constantly increased taxes to cover its perennial budget deficits. New products were found for taxation, and new taxes devised for old products. The Sugar Taxation Act, the Molasses Act and many others were passed, but none was observed conscientiously, and all such impositions were evaded as far as possible in every conceivable way. Irate resistance to the taxes escalated: street fights with tax collectors and tax stamp agents became a common sight, demonstrations were held, merchants formed opposition associations. The first inter-colony Congress was held, boycotts were imposed, and trade with the mother country declined steeply, as did government revenues.

Events took a more violent turn in Boston in March 1770. A playful snowballing of a troop of Redcoats developed into an angry mob attack. It was repulsed by fire and in the aftermath of what came to be known as the Boston Massacre, several Bostonians lay dead. In full accord with the general mood, popular leaders like Samuel Adams, who were organized as the self-styled 'Sons of Liberty', were soon accusing London of harboring 'malicious designs' on American liberty.

Plantation farmers in the south were suffocating under the load of their debts to British merchants; in the north the multiplying duties and taxes were stifling the colonists; and all of them sorely wanted to go west. Liberal spirits like Benjamin Franklin and the intellectuals emerging from Harvard College (founded in 1636) and the six other colleges established in rapid succession between 1740 and 1770, stoked the controversy and gave voice to the implicit demands of the revolutionary atmosphere, which lacked only a spark.

*An Indian village in Florida, after
a drawing by the French Hugenot Jacques
Le Moyne de Morgues, whose materials
were a major inspiration for T. de Bry.*

THE FLAMES OF INDEPENDENCE were ignited by the famous Boston Tea Party on December 16, 1773, when a group of Adams' supporters, disguised as Mohawk Indians, boarded three British ships at anchor and dumped their cargoes of tea into Boston harbor, in protest against the British government's manipulations with the tea tax. The Crown took a firm stand, sending in the soldiery and closing down the port of Boston until the tea was 'properly paid'. At the same time, the British passed the Quebec Act, which virtually deprived the Americans of any right to colonization north of the Ohio, tightened the autocratic regime, and consolidated the position of the Catholic Church in Canada. The Americans declared these and related acts 'intolerable', and resolved that no obedience was due them. They proceeded to summon representatives of all the colonies to the 'first Continental Congress' held in Philadelphia on September 5, 1774. The rising tensions culminated on April 19, 1775, at Lexington and Concord, near Boston. Two hundred British soldiers were killed in clashes with American militiamen. The War of Independence thus begun was to rage for almost seven years.

In actual fact, America's independent course was not clearly charted until the year after the outbreak of war, when a committee led by Thomas Jefferson, one of the pleiad of notables in the vanguard of the revolutionary ferment, drafted the Declaration of Independence. Adopted by the Continental Congress on July 4, 1776, it formally announced that "it becomes necessary for one people to dissolve the political bonds which have connected them with another, and to assume, among the powers of the earth, the separate and equal station to which the laws of nature and of nature's God entitle them."

In a few simple, dignified sentences the Declaration reflects the fundamental tenets of Enlightenment philosophy. "We hold these truths to be self-evident. That all men are created equal; that they are endowed by their Creator with certain unalienable rights; that among these are life, liberty, and the pursuit of happiness; that, to secure these rights, governments are instituted among men... that whenever any form of government becomes destructive of these ends, it is the right of the people to alter or to abolish it, and to institute new government, laying its foundation on such principles, and organizing its powers in such form as to them shall seem most likely to effect their safety and happiness..." The Declaration then gives a long list of complaints against the 'absolute tyranny' of the King of Great Britain, the repeated 'injuries and usurpations' committed by him. It concludes with the proclamation that the "United Colonies are, and of right ought to be, FREE AND INDEPENDENT STATES... absolved from all allegiance to the British Crown... with the full power to levy war, conclude peace, contract alliances, establish commerce, and do all other acts and things which independent states may of right do."

But the war against the British dragged on: neither of the belligerents could muster sufficient military clout to deal a decisive blow. Although Britain was superior in military might throughout, it was not able to rout the American forces under the command of George Washington or to maintain control over the greater part of the land. The decisive victory went to the Americans with the surrender of Lord Cornwallis in Virginia in 1781. They had had the help of the French, who provided financial and military assistance, partly in reprisal against the British for the defeat of France in 1763, and partly because the ideals enshrined in the Declaration of Independence, conveyed to Paris by Benjamin Franklin in person, had fired the imagination of French intellectuals.

THE DEMOCRATIC IDEAS which stemmed from the belief in inalienable rights enshrined in the Declaration of Independence, were a strong motive force in the struggle against the British. Many of the heads of state congresses and local committees endeavored to put them into practice, while aristocratic elements, including loyalists faithful to the British, remained indifferent. In these revolutionary years there was considerable chaos – courts were clogged or did not sit, debts were not paid, loyalists were terrorized, tarred and feathered. The first central government of the United States tried somehow to combine liberty with a semblance of order, and local self-government with state unity, but the confederation remained only a union, and power was retained by the member states. In the words of George Washington: the states were united only by a 'rope of sand'.

The process of adjustment did not move at the same pace in the different states. Extension of the right to vote proceeded vigorously in Pennsylvania, where the new constitution, furthermore, vested greater power in the legislature than in the executive branch, as was also the case in New Hampshire, Delaware, North Carolina and Georgia. On the other hand, the aristocracy or upper classes managed to retain greater authority in Massachusetts, New York, Virginia and South Carolina. The trend to democratization underlay the confiscation of loyalists' estates, as well as the abolition of church privileges, a step which contributed to intellectual freedom.

The liberal idealism of the revolutionary period gave impetus to the movement to abolish slavery. In Massachusetts all slaves were declared free the very year the war with the British came to a close. In the South, things moved more slowly and all states went only so far as to ban the importation of new slaves, preferring instead to postpone the abolition of slavery.

Each of the states in the confederation had a single vote. A majority of nine votes was required for passage of a bill, but the full accord of all thirteen states was necessary to amend a bill that had already been passed. This complex mechanism was considered by many to be too cumbersome and one of the reasons for the ineffectiveness of the new national government. A small but highly influential group began to lobby for the creation of 'a more efficient federal state', one that would be 'adequate to the exigencies of the Union'. They argued that the country needed unity and discipline more than it needed wider liberties. They sought a stronger national government to take control of the country's major problems: it had fallen heavily into debt and was hurriedly printing money; the need to provide adequate defense and to protect trade had become apparent; and the country sorely lacked a merchant navy.

THE PROMULGATION OF THE 1787 CONSTITUTION was supposed to put an end to 'a time of disorder and democratic foolishness' and to help consolidate the situation and build the foundations of independence. The 'supreme law' was the product of reasoned wisdom and compromise between the interests of the North and the South, between the several large and the many small member states.

To 'form a more perfect union, establish justice, insure domestic tranquility, provide for the common defense, promote the general welfare, and secure the blessings of liberty to ourselves and our posterity', the Founding Fathers drew on both the centuries-long English experience in government and the legal traditions which had taken shape under the circumstances peculiar to the New World. The framers of the Constitution, which is one of the shortest if not *the* shortest document of its kind in the world, were also inspired by contemporary currents in European political theory, the Enlightenment, and growing social idealism. They were particularly concerned that the new social system should be based on the principle that each citizen had a right to live in freedom and to dispose of the goods he had obtained as a result of his own work or by inheritance. They fully accepted, moreover, the French philosopher Montesquieu's argument that the best safeguard against potential tyranny was a clearcut division of power. Farsightedly, they carefully chose their words to ensure that the open-minded code they had drawn up might later be broadened and supplemented.

The final passage and ratification of the Constitution of the United States of America was completed in 1789. The Bill of Rights was incorporated two years later, in 1791. The ten amendments that make up the Bill were a distillation of the experience of 'oppressive rule down the centuries' and were designed to forestall the 'danger of tyranny in government'. The amendments proclaim the freedom of religion, speech and the press; the right to public assembly and to present petitions to the government for the redress of grievances; they guarantee that 'no person shall be deprived of life, freedom or property' without due process of law and public trial, and assure the security of the individual and his property.

The Bill of Rights has been acclaimed the whole world over and it would be hard to find a national constitution that does not outwardly endorse these same rights, regardless of the system of government. The interpretation of these rights has, of course, evolved with time. When they were first framed, their primary purpose was to protect the majority from the tyranny of the minority in power, and they were less concerned with civil rights in the modern sense of protecting individuals or minorities with views or interests that differ from those of the majority. With its deeper, extended meaning, the Bill of Rights is just as relevant today, and not only in the United States. It may often happen that rights have been violated or abused. But at least they have been laid down and recognized as rights. All that remains to be done is to fight for their observance.

For Americans in general, the government (with its 200-year-old, greatly supplemented and amended Constitution) only provides the legal framework and a degree of public order, leaving individuals free to run their own lives. A wide variety of 'freedoms' have sprung up on the 'pastless' soil of the United States. They go far beyond the freedoms *from*, uppermost in the minds of the authors of the Bill of Rights, and include an array of freedoms *to*. As the American commentator Lance Morrow notes, Americans would need about 500 different words for freedom to express all the subtleties of tone, depth and temperature that have become associated with it. Just as the Eskimos have 100 different words for snow.

TWO HUNDRED YEARS AFTER the adoption of the United States Constitution, its principles are unchanged. The Constitution provides the blueprint for the governmental system. The form of government is based on three fundamental principles: federalism, the separation of powers, and respect for the Constitution and the rule of law. Each citizen is subject to two governments: that of the state and that of the Union. The primary function of the state is to assure law and order and to provide education and public health, welfare and other general public services. The Union, or the federal government, is responsible for foreign affairs, defense, and matters of common interest to all the states, including domestic commerce. The scope of the federal government has expanded in response to the demand by most, if not all of the states for assistance in such areas as the social services, education, research, and the like. In many cases this expansion was carried out by means of explicit amendment of the Constitution. In some cases, however, it has issued from looseness in the Constitution's working, making possible new interpretations. As the system of government has developed and the Union has grown, so too has federal power.

At both state and federal levels, power is divided among three institutions: the executive (the President or Governor), the legislature (Congress with its upper house, the Senate, and lower house, the House of Representatives, and usually bicameral state parliaments), and the judiciary. The three branches of government are arrayed as checks and balances to each other. The same pattern is repeated at county level within the states. The counties are further divided into municipalities. There are nearly 20,000 municipalities in the United States with their own local forms of government.

Article II of the United States Constitution invests executive power in the President, who is elected for a four-year term. Presidential elections have been held regularly every four years without a break. The original rules are still in force concerning eligibility for President. The candidate must not be younger than 35 years, must be a natural-born American citizen, and must have lived in the United States for at least 14 years. From the outset, the Constitution has allowed a sitting President, Vice-President and any civil officer of the United States to be removed from office before term by an impeachment process. To deal with specific areas of national and international affairs the executive has 13 different departments – State, Treasury, Defense, etc. In addition, numerous independent agencies have been established to carry out special functions.

According to the Constitution, all men are equal before the law and are equally entitled to its protection. Similarly, all states are equal and none can receive special consideration from the federal government. When a state constitution or law passed by a state legislature or by the national Congress, conflicts with the Constitution, it is null and void. Decisions handed down by the Supreme Court over the course of the past two centuries have confirmed and strengthened this doctrine of constitutional supremacy.

Twenty-four amendments have been made to the Constitution in all. Those subsequent to the Bill of Rights cover a wide range of subjects – the prohibition of slavery; protection of the right to vote against discrimination based on race, color, sex or previous condition of servitude; changes in the system of presidential elections; affirmation of the right to vote despite failure to pay a poll tax, etc.

The supreme law of the country has certainly been implemented in close correlation with developments in American society, domestic growth and the country's affirmation in the international arena. At the time when it was adopted, the country was primarily concerned with defeating the French and the British, and almost as much with subduing the Indians. Then came years of conflict with Tunisia, Tripoli and Algeria over pirate attacks on United States shipping. Just how much power the federal government needed, and how much it lacked may be appreciated from the course of events after the prohibition of the importation of slaves: although the decree was passed in 1808, a further 250,000 slaves had been imported by 1860.

During this time the Spanish withdrew from Florida. Another ten states had joined the Union by 1840, and the western border of the United States then ran down through Ohio, Missouri and Arkansas. Six years later Mexico was forced to concede Texas, Arizona, New Mexico, Nevada and part of Colorado, and a bargain was struck with the British over the border in Oregon. While revolution was raging in Europe in 1848, America was shaking with gold fever: in a single year 80,000 people rushed to California.

The soaring number of immigrants and very high birth rate caused a rapid growth in the population: by the middle of the nineteenth century the United States already had more than 31 million people. The biggest surge occurred in the northern, more economically propulsive, free states, which were advancing more rapidly than the predominantly agricultural, slave-holding south. The growing friction between the two did not abate: while the northern and most of the newly-acceded states prohibited slavery, the South refused to relinquish it.

Historians differ somewhat on the question of the 'principal' reason for the Civil War which broke out in 1861, just nine years after Harriet Beecher

79. *Man's efforts seem puny when compared with the imposing sculptures carved from the hills and deserts by the elements. No longer barriers on the east-west trail, now they are just rather intimidating reminders. Only a few pioneers, compelled by illness, fatigue or some other pressing circumstance, ventured to put down stakes in these parts. That is, until the gold fever became an epidemic.*

80.   More than 100 million years ago, titanic forces folded and compressed the Rockies. These tremendous movements of the earth and the action of the sun and atmospherics are continuing today. Their creative talents are astounding.

81.   Besides such sightseeing 'musts' as the Colorado plateau and the Grand Canyon, 4,000–5,000 feet deep and 217 miles long, the wild, untouched parts of the majestic Rocky Mountains, off the beaten track, have been gaining in popularity with holidaymakers.

82.   When molten rock was forced to the surface it brought up gold, copper, lead, silver, molybdenum and other valuable minerals. Although these parts are among the most richly endowed with natural resources, federal government policy has wisely promoted diversification of the economy.

83. At the beginning of the eighties, the US census showed that the American Indian population numbered only about 1,534,000, much less than when Europeans first began to settle. The American Indian was granted US citizenship, by special law of Congress, only in 1924. About a million now live on some 270 reservations, which have been established in 26 states. In remote rural areas, where most reservations are located, the general store is still the main supplier of daily needs.

84. Vast tracts of land were taken from the Indians, primarily because of the great natural wealth they represented. Litigation to reclaim the land or gain compensation has been slow, to say the least. A claim for the loss of the Black Hills of South Dakota presented by the Sioux Indian nation was recently upheld: in 1980, the Supreme Court ordered the US Government to pay 117 million dollars, plus interest, in compensation. Many similar cases are still pending.

85.   The unemployment rate among the Indians in the late seventies was almost 40 percent, and the average per capita income on large Indian reservations was well below the US poverty line.

86.   The latest data show that on some small Indian reservations as many as 65 percent are unemployed. Some enterprising Indians on reservations near big cities or tourist resorts earn a livelihood by putting on displays of traditional customs and skills.

87

89

87. Will this little Indian girl go to university one day? Who can tell. In the late seventies, though, the high school dropout rate among American Indians averaged 53 percent.

88. A survey made after World War II showed that nine out of ten Indians lived in substandard housing, and the situation is probably not much better today. Indian city-dwellers usually congregate in the poor 'red' ghettos.

89. Their poverty and displacement may account for the fact that the incidence of alcoholism and tuberculosis is highest among American Indians. An attempt is being made to restore their self-confidence and well-being by fostering their cultural heritage and customs, though it seems questionable whether these can survive for much longer in an age of urbanization and technology.

91

90. Over the past few decades the ire of young Indians has been no less intense than that of young blacks. Their new militancy erupted in November 1969, when a small group seized Alcatraz Island in San Francisco Bay, and then again two years later, when members of the American Indian Movement took eleven people hostage at Wounded Knee in South Dakota, site of a massacre of Sioux Indians in 1890.

91. In the fifties and sixties, Indians began to move into urban centers, particularly after 1953 when Congress adopted a policy terminating the status of certain tribes as

wards of the US Government. While many have remained faithful to the customs and dress of their ancestors, those living in cities have to forego their traditional ways.

92. The disenchanted urbanized American Indian is left with the dream of returning to his people, and the legends of brave ancestors who were no match for the intruding settlers.

Stowe wrote *Uncle Tom's Cabin*. In the North they called it the 'War of the Rebellion' because seven southern states had founded a separate Confederate States of America and seceded from the Union. In the South they called it the 'War between the States'. Its causes were deep-rooted and intricately intertwined, and particular political, economic or social factors cannot easily be singled out. Political irresponsibility and the fanaticism of inveterate rivals certainly contributed their part. Nevertheless, it was crucial that the North, a free society of small-holdings and businesses and flourishing industries, was developing faster than the South, which decided on a final gamble.

The carnage lasted four years. It took 600,000 lives in the North and as many as 900,000 in the South. This savage war pitted 'the feelings and convictions of one form of society against another form of society', as one contemporary described this 'tragic inevitability'. Finally, drawing on its intrinsic dynamism which had become synonymous with economic efficiency, the North carried off the victory.

The brutalities committed in Florida, carried out under the command of Hernando de Soto, were recorded by the superb artist-engraver Theodore de Bry, whose America *collection depicted 35 subjects covering a span of 150 years (1590–1634).*

93. The suicide rate is higher among American Indians than in other ethnic groups. There is no doubt that of all the positive aspects of current social integration processes, the best defense against alienation lies in the strengthening of ethnic roots and sense of identity. A long road lies ahead.

A LAND OF CHANGE

PARADOXICAL AS IT MAY SOUND, the fundamental constant of the 200-year-old political system of the United States has been and still is, change itself.

Thomas Paine, author and standard-bearer of the American Revolution, raised a storm with his rejection of monarchy as a pagan invention just a few months before the 'eruption' in 1776. To the thousands of predominantly religious Americans that avidly read his essay *Common Sense*, he carried the message that they must, first and foremost, listen to the command of God, not King. This was a ready-made justification for rushing to the barricades of the American Revolution – all that was to ensue bore the seal of Providence. Inescapable personal tragedies assumed a deeper significance on the broad, national plane: in the great open country the servants of God were multiplying and becoming economically stronger. To succeed, to contribute to the commonweal, was not only an exalted act of patriotism, but divinely ordained.

The Founding Fathers – George Washington, Thomas Jefferson, Alexander Hamilton, John Adams and the 'oldest and probably the wisest of them all', Benjamin Franklin – and the many others that rallied to them were not driven primarily by religious convictions. But they were all imbued with the Protestant ethic and its moral precepts and system of values. Its rationale bent, and the commonsense inquiries of the Enlightenment gave wing to impassioned and unflagging drive. The visionary quality of the dreamer was married to the realism of the down-to-earth pragmatist.

The rigid social systems of the various European countries the immigrants had left behind and, as Americans, rejected, were based on sharp lines of distinction between the nobility, the merchants, the landed gentry, craftsmen and peasants, and wide inequality of rights. By contrast, colonial and later independent America was a land of great social mobility. Benjamin Franklin, an enlightened and witty writer, scientist and America's first diplomat, put this succinctly when he warned that those 'with no virtues other than their ancestry' had nothing to seek in America. There the so-called virtues of lineage could not secure a position or remuneration. Whoever has tried it has failed, Franklin said, explaining to the astounded French that in America the cropfarmer and mechanic were valued because their work was 'useful'.

A NEW AMERICAN MAN was perceived by Crevecoeur, who served as French Consul in New York. In 1782 he described the changes the newcomer to America displayed: "A European, when he first arrives, seems limited in his intentions, as well as in his views, but he very suddenly alters his scale... The American is a new man who acts upon new principles, he must therefore entertain their ideas and form new opinions. [The American] is either a European or a descendant of a European, hence that strange mixture of blood which you will find in no other country. He no sooner breathes our air than he forms schemes and embarks on designs he never would have conceived in his own country."

Since Americans were starting from scratch, historians meticulously recorded every event or discovery that propelled the nation forward, starting from Benjamin Franklin and his electrical experiments. Although he is still regarded as one of America's great pure scientists, he gave mankind such practical everyday inventions as the lightning rod, in 1752.

Forty years later, in 1793, cotton farming in the south was revolutionized by Eli Whitney's cotton gin, which mechanically separated the cotton from the seeds and hulls. The consequent increase in productivity and profits encouraged big landowners to buy out small farmers and enlarge their plantations. It also indirectly underpinned a boom in slave labor, and spurred on development of the textile industry already taking root in the north. As is often the case, Whitney himself apparently derived little benefit from his device. He had better luck when he designed a gun with interchangeable parts which could be produced by machines instead of by hand. However, it took another twenty years for these fundamental principles of mass production, termed the 'American system', to become established.

One of the most important events of the epoch was Robert Foulton's innovative use, in 1808, of Watts' steam engine to power ships. Prior to this, in 1785, John Fitch had constructed a quite workable steamship driven by steam-powered oars. Although he gained exclusive rights to shipping lines around New York and to most of the Atlantic states, he could not find the capital backing he needed and in deep frustration committed suicide. Foulton was more fortunate. His first round trip from New York to Albany ushered in the era of the conquest of the American waterways.

The Industrial Revolution was already well underway in Great Britain and had begun to spread to western Europe by the third quarter of the nineteenth century. It had also just reached the United States, where it found immensely congenial ground: vast natural resources and a highly receptive attitude. The budding nation with its strong pioneering spirit which stressed individual initiative, coupled with organized government protection and promotion of enterprise, set itself ambitious goals. Businessmen came from all walks of life, and those that succeeded were not usually noted for their moral qualms in their dealings. But the historian Henry B. Parkes points out that they 'believed they were working for progress and were carrying out God's will', and adds wryly that it would be foolish to harbor too many moral scruples in achieving such noble ends.

The vigorous development of the transportation network was a great boon to the spread of the industrial revolution throughout the United States of America. It had been necessitated in the first place by the great distances to be traversed by those eager to tap the country's untouched resources for export, long before national industries had begun to mushroom. The intensive and early investment in transport was also pushed along by the rapid growth in population and the press to move to ever-new areas: the new American man was in a hurry to hit the trail...

FLATBOATS THAT COULD SAIL ON A HEAVY DEW, as the wisecrack of the time claimed, were a special type of steamboat designed to sail on shallow waters. The steamboat was one mode of transport that burgeoned particularly rapidly in the early 1800s. The first Mississippi steamboat was built in Pittsburg in 1811, and it was only a short time before the river was turned into a busy thoroughfare carrying a constant flow of cargo and passengers. In the fierce competition for business there were collisions, boiler explosions and many other accidents. Statistics of the time show there had been more than 1,000 ships wrecked by the middle of the century. The first federal traffic regulations were passed to bring some order to the scene.

Mark Twain and the gifted cineasts of later generations have immortalized cruises down the Mississippi, usually on very sumptuous riverboats, and help us to realize just how vital the waterways were in that age. It is not so well-known, however, that the first hard-surfaced road was built in the United States in 1794, linking Philadelphia and Lancaster in Pennsylvania. Or that over 40 million dollars had been spent on road-building by 1812. As a rule, roads and bridges were built by private companies which operated them as toll collectors. Often the profits from the roads turned out to be too low and the companies abandoned incompleted routes to the federal or state government.

While the automobile was still a long way from the horizon, the first American steamship, the *Savannah*, set off in 1819 across the Atlantic, bound for Liverpool. Unfurling its sails at times, it made the trip in twenty-nine days. This was the time of the great opening of the United States toward Europe, as well as the opening up of the interior of the continent.

America's great canal-building fever broke out in the 1820s, starting with the construction of the visionary and highly successful Erie Canal. This 339-mile man-made link between Buffalo and the Hudson River was finished in seven years, opening in 1825. This masterful stroke shortened the journey from New York to Buffalo on Lake Erie from twenty to a mere six days and reduced transport costs from $100 to just $5. It was instrumental in propelling New York ahead of Philadelphia and Boston, and naturally was eagerly copied elsewhere, in a frenzy of canal-building. By 1850 almost 3,750 miles of canals had been dug in various parts of the country. Of course, not all survived the advent of the railroads and highways. Parallel with this, shipbuilding began to flourish. Giant sailing ships were built, capable of crossing the Atlantic in only thirteen days.

Meanwhile railroad construction made rapid progress and was boosted even more by canal fever. Baltimore was linked by rail with Ohio by the 1830s. In competition with the British, the Americans began to build their own locomotives. The expansion of the railroad system brought other Atlantic cities back into the race with New York. All-in-all, river transport stimulated road and rail development and *vice versa*, and together it all had a major impact on the quality and price of transport services. The country was ever more closely interconnected as the railroad network advanced by leaps and bounds. The total length of railroads in 1850 was 8,700 miles. In the following decade, it grew to an impressive 28,000 miles.

The development of the telegraph in the United States was just as dynamic. The inventor of the magnetic telegraph, Samuel Morse, sent the first telegram from Washington to Baltimore in 1844, saying drolly, 'What hath God wrought.' Sixteen years later, 46,500 miles of telegraph lines snaked across the country. The following year, 1861, the continent was bridged and the east and west coasts of the United States were linked. The transatlantic cable, allowing instant communication with the other side of the Atlantic, was laid in 1866. Just three years later, in spite of the continuing Civil War, another transportation peak was reached: the first transcontinental railway line was completed.

INVENTIVENESS AND MOBILITY transformed the country. A handful of basic inventions fundamentally altered the conditions of growth. The land of the Central Plains, for example, remained unyielding until the 1830s, when the appearance of the steel plow made it possible to turn the soil efficiently, and the prairies became the granary of the United States. New machines and equipment were developed in rapid succession: McCormick started up industrial production of a harvester and promoted sales by giving credit which the farmers could repay after the harvest; Elias Hove invented the sewing machine; Edwin Drake devised the first commercial oil-pump in 1858...

Wandering livestock was a constant bane, particularly for homesteaders trying to establish farms on the open range. Wood for fencing was in very short supply and therefore expensive. Joseph Glidden, an Illinois farmer, resolved the problem in 1874 by inventing barbed wire, and within a few years his company was manufacturing over 600 miles of wire a day. In the same part of the country, the introduction of windmills to draw up deep-level underground water for crop farming marked the beginning of another stage...

Patently, the habits and customs built up in the process of settling the continent, as historian Henry B. Parkes notes, together with the qualities of seventeenth-century Calvinism and eighteenth-century Liberalism, combined to shape a national ethos which extolled the successful entrepreneur as the most valuable member of society. Entrepreneurs with the necessary ability, initiative, energy and driving ambition undertook the job of mobilizing national resources and production forces, and organizing the construction of railroads and factories.

The five-fold increase in the railroad network in the thirty years following the Civil War turned it into a fresh source of wealth and accelerated the growth of coal mining, steel works and other industries. At the turn of the twentieth century, the United States produced more steel than Britain and Germany together. Output of oil and oil products grew apace. Following the discoveries of Thomas A. Edison and George Westinghouse, the use of electricity for lighting, engine-power and transport spread rapidly. Next came the invention of the telephone, in 1876.

The typewriter, adding machine, refrigerator, cash register and many others were major innovations. The style of life was changed by the development of new methods of conserving foodstuffs, which in turn stimulated agriculture, vinegrowing, livestock farming and fishing.

The last decade of the nineteenth century saw the first execution in the electric chair – the first legal electrocution. In 1893, the dynamo was exhibited for the first time at the World Fair in New York, and immediately began to be installed in hydroelectric power plants. Three years later, electric current powered the screening of Thomas Edison's motion picture at its world premiere in New York City. The early years of the twentieth century brought interest in the study of industrial operations in order to raise productivity. Then Henry Ford invented the moving assembly line, lowering the costs of automobile production and leading the way in mass industrial production. "I am going to democratize the automobile," he declared. "When I'm through, everybody will be able to afford one, and about everybody will have one." And this is precisely what he did – by turning out identical automobiles by the millions. He compressed the working day into just eight hours and doubled wages at the same time. Automobile output soared. Another vital contribution to mass production techniques had been made a decade or so earlier by Frederic W. Taylor, a Midvale Steel Company engineer, who analyzed 'how quickly the various kinds of work... ought to be done'. His studies made scientific management a national obsession.

Meanwhile, aviation was making its way to center stage. The Wright brothers took wing in their airplanes in 1903. That same year an automobile crossed the continent, from San Francisco to New York, in 69 days, from May 23 to August 1. It was only another eight years before the first transcontinental flight was made: Galbraith P. Rogers flew the distance from New York to California in 68 days, with an elapsed time of 49 hours.

PRESERVING PEACE WITH HONOR having become impossible and contradictory, President Woodrow Wilson declared America's entry into the

Theodore de Bry produced many renderings of the Spanish conquest of the New World.

First World War on April 6, 1917. The war became a new driving force for the whole of the American economy. Industry shifted to war production in a very short span of time. One of the first objects was to build a 'bridge' to France: two new ships were to replace very Allied vessel sunk by the Germans. Industrial manufacturing was improved in these years by thousands of innovations. But the United States' entry into the war did more than alter production plans: it radically changed the situation on the front lines. Ultimately the Germans were forced to capitulate.

The postwar years were marked by booming prosperity, galloping industrial, agricultural and overall progress. Aviation may be taken as an example: air mail delivery became a regular service after the first postal flight in 1918. In 1927, Charles A. Lindberg crossed the Atlantic in a non-stop flight from New York to Paris.

It seemed that everything was possible, that anything could change, and vast sums of money began to pour into the new front-running industries. Enterprising people turned to new challenges, new professions, new quests. But then came something that no one had forecast: the Great Depression. Historians call this economic collapse 'the Panic of 1929' and link it to earlier panics in the recurrent boom-bust cycles in the US economy. But this time it was no ordinary bust; it was not a common cold the economy had caught, but full-blown pneumonia. Moreover, the rest of the world ended up doing much more than just sneezing.

As the crisis dragged on for years, new ways of handling it had to be devised. But the old American motto still applied: everything can change. President Franklin Roosevelt inaugurated the New Deal. The federal government launched massive public works programs and a full-scale overhaul and reform of the banking system to foster economic recovery.

Instead of hesitating, they hurried into action, but recovery was no quick process. By some accounts it took up to 1937, while by others it was the Second World War that finally pulled the United States out of the crisis.

Tobacco was used as a medicinal as well as for smoking. Woodcut by Girolamo Benzoni, 1565.

FORGING A NATION

THE CHIEF MIDWIVES AT THE BIRTH OF THE AMERICAN NATION were the industrial revolution, immigration and the growth of the cities. The prevailing atmosphere was one of infinite trust in the divine right of capital and strict application of the principles of *laissez-faire*, the doctrine that an economic system functions best when the government interferes least. In the period following the Declaration of Independence, when the population ranged around four million, the rate of immigration averaged about 5,000 a year until the 1820s. Since some four-fifths of the population, the nucleus of the Union, were English-speaking, the newcomers generally blended easily into the community and took on its characteristics. The process was all the smoother since the new arrivals were still coming predominantly from Great Britain and Ireland, and only to a lesser extent from northern Europe. Consequently they mostly shared a common language and similar goals and ideals with the 'Americans' they joined.

A turning point came in the early 1830s with a steep rise in the number of immigrants, particularly Germans and Scandinavians. They tended to head off west, acquiring land and equipment on credit from the railways or big land-owning companies. They first moved into the wide expanses of the Central Lowlands and then went directly west. The pathfinders before them had usually spread in gradually from adjacent areas in the east, creeping steadily across the continent. Here too the newcomers mainly encountered English speakers. The number of settlers in these parts multiplied rapidly in spite of the harsh climate with its long cold winters, hot dry summers, recurrent droughts and unrelenting winds. From 1860 to 1900, for example, the population in Kansas, Nebraska, Dakota, Iowa and Minnesota grew seven-fold, from just under one million to more than seven million people.

The egalitarian processes unfolding on American soil on the eve of and following the election of President Andrew Jackson (1828–1836) played a major part in encouraging immigrants. Jackson's ideas of egalitarian democracy evoked an eager response among the humble folk of Europe. Another major cause of the influx was the dire living conditions in the Old World at that time. The development of shipping was one more factor. The vigorous rise in American exports outpaced by far the growth in imports, and shipping agents began offering low-fare passage in makeshift berths in the empty ship holds on the return journey to America. Traveling conditions were unsuitable, trying and often downright unhygienic – disease and even deaths were not uncommon among the passengers. Foul weather could stretch out the voyage in sailing ships from one to as many as three months, in which case food, water and medicine would run precariously low. Nonetheless, the holds of cotton ships returning to New Orleans were soon crowded with German and French migrants, who later transferred to paddle steamers on the Mississippi to reach destinations like Cincinatti, St Louis or Milwaukee.

The breweries of German beers in the latter two cities are reminders of these early travelers.

In these years, Irish immigrants came to the promised land in the holds of lumber ships. Their point of disembarkation was usually determined by the location of the ship's next cargo for Europe, but more often than not it was Boston. Industry was only beginning to flourish and the largely unskilled Irish took up manual work, often dangerous construction jobs. Many stayed on in Boston, while others set out along the canals and railroads in quest of opportunity.

The Irish crossed the ocean to escape the grinding poverty of their homeland and the oppression of the English landowners who extorted exorbitant rents and dues, heedless of their terrible penury. According to official records, in one community of 9,000 people, for example, there were only ten beds to be counted, while four five-member families did not even own a chair. In the 1840s, a million people died of starvation in Ireland. Those who made it to the shores of the United States hurriedly sent passage money home to family and friends. But the going was by no means easy in predominantly Protestant America either. Many factories posted warning signs: 'No Irish Need Apply'. Unlike the Protestant Germans, who quickly absorbed much of American culture, despite the fact that they tended to cluster together fairly compactly and retained their sense of national identity, the often fiercely Catholic Irish did not assimilate so well.

THE GEOGRAPHIC DISTRIBUTION OF ETHNIC GROUPS in the United States of America was dictated by numerous historical factors, which caused the main bodies of each group to arrive at different times, and to concentrate in areas where opportunities were then available. At the time when migrants were streaming into America from England, Ireland and northwestern Europe, people living in other parts of Europe, and even Africa and Asia, were probably just as willing to become Americans. But the great bulk of freighters that offered cheap passage traveled along routes to northern and western Europe, and proper passenger berths on sailing ships were few in number and expensive.

The advent of the steamship, which became a common sight on the Atlantic after the 1840s, brought a real revolution in this respect, as Thomas Sowell of Harvard University's Hoover Institute notes. To promote business, the proliferating steamship companies coaxed adventurous spirits from all over Europe to escape poverty and often religious, national or political oppression, and flock to the land of 'freedom and equality'. The sea voyage had been shortened to about ten days, although conditions were still unacceptable by modern standards. There was soon a swelling number of travelers from southern and eastern Europe, who differed markedly from the earlier immigrants and the 'average' American in both cultural and religious traditions.

This growing influx spurred the settlement of the western half of the American continent, which was opened up by the incorporation of new territories – by force of persuasion – culminating in the purchase of Alaska in 1867. Incredible as it may seem, the same generation that built the railroads, roads and canals, that instituted the telegraph and new industries across the continent, also occupied more land in just thirty years than had been settled in the previous two-and-a-half centuries. In order to squeeze out the Indians, they frequently resorted to dirty tactics, breaking treaties and violating recognized property rights. Besides directly forcing the Indians off their land, in a quarter of a century the 'paleface' virtually exterminated some 13 million buffalo in the West, thereby destroying the foundations of the Plains Indians' civilization.

Statistics show that more than a million people entered the United

98

94–99.   Tourism is opening up more and more areas of exceptional primeval beauty. Movie-makers who first chose these parts as spectacular settings for their films deserve much of the credit for their popularity.

99

101

100–101. The wild places of their homeland hold a compelling attraction for Americans, relatively few of whom vacation abroad. Every year some 42 million people visit the national parks, not to mention the many other scenic areas all over the USA.

102

102–103.   The long lines of hopeful gold-diggers had to have food. Once they set up their camps in the wilderness, farming soon got under way. The remote, picturesque villages that grew up in those times have preserved the tranquility of yesteryear even though eight railway lines and a dozen highways have superceded the old pioneer trails.

104–104A.   Driven away from the East, the heretical Mormons, or Latter-Day Saints, finally found their promised land in the wilds of the Great Salt Lake area, where they helped found the state of Utah.

06

105–107. *Following in the footsteps of the Mormons, latter-day heretics, dismayed by the life of divisive competition and crass consumerism, come to these same parts in search of a secluded valley. Roaming through Utah and other mountain states in their odd caravans, they eventually find sites for their new communes.*

107

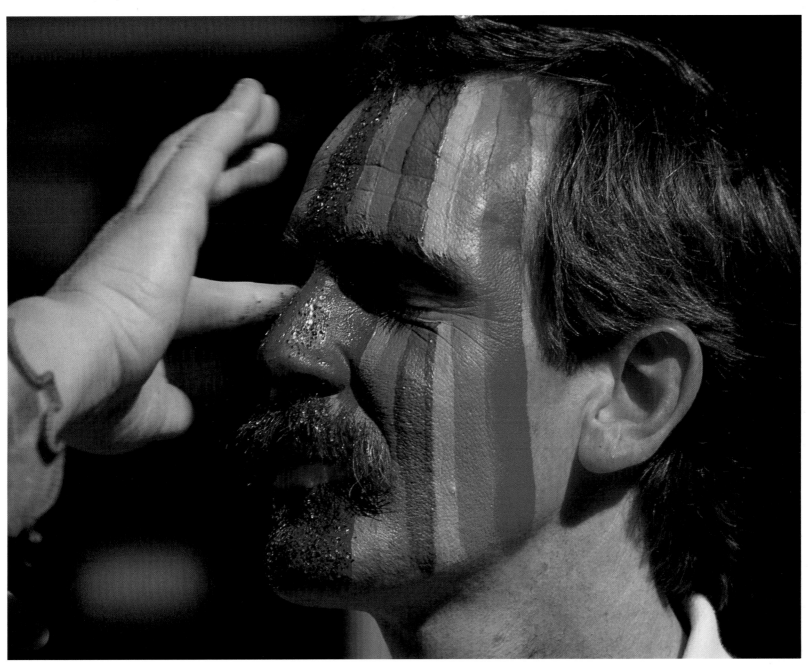

108–109.   *People seek their happiness in all sorts of places and all kinds of ways. Though rainbows may promise happiness, they do not always bring it. Nevertheless, the shimmering sands of Nevada and the brilliant lights of Las Vegas carry all the allure of a pot of gold for a great many.*

States between 1820 and 1840, or four times more than in the previous twenty years. During the next forty years to 1880, newcomers poured in at a rate of a quarter of a million each year, or fifty times faster than at the beginning of the century. By the middle of the nineteenth century, the population of the United States was already greater than that of any country in Europe. By 1880 the young country had around 50 million inhabitants.

This was a critical juncture: whereas in the mid-1880s 'new arrivals' were in the minority and 'old' Americans made up the bulk of the population, by the end of the century large communities had sprung up in which the majority of the adults were European-born. One of human society's greatest dramas began to unfold.

THE RISE OF AMERICAN NATIONAL AWARENESS, which set its historical stamp on this drama, was precipitated by the inrush of newcomers. The flow did not falter in the slightest even during the calamitous years of the Civil War (1861–65), when the main issue at stake was whether the Union would be cut in two. Since most of the newcomers disembarked at northern ports, they tended to side with the North against division of the nation. They joined its military operations against the South, which in a sense was a foreign country to them, under the banner of 'conscious Americans'.

Once the Civil War came to an end, the American economy started to blossom on an unprecedented scale. The massive movement to the United States threatened to become a serious drain on some European countries. In the 1890s, for example, a tenth of the entire populations of Sweden and Norway fled the grim poverty prevalent there. In just the first fourteen years of the twentieth century, up to the outbreak of the First World War, 12 million Europeans poured into the United States. Two million came from Italy alone in just one decade. Migrants began to stream in from the Austro-Hungarian Empire and Russia. This new wave brought Czechs, Slovaks, Poles, Ukrainians, Jews, Hungarians, Croats, Serbs, Slovenes and many others. Several million came to stay only temporarily, returning after a few years, but more than 20 million of the 26 million immigrants that flooded the country between 1870 and 1920 stayed on to make America their new home. The peak inflow occurred in 1907, when exactly 1,285,349 immigrants entered the United States of America.

To a great extent each ethnic group had its characteristic period of entry and place of settlement. The Scandinavians and Germans put down roots mostly in the upper northwest; the Chinese and Japanese, along the west coast; the Irish and Scots in the Appalachians; Cuban refugees in Florida; the Jews, Italians and the Irish along the east coast, in New York in particular. Immigrants from eastern Europe concentrated in the areas of the coal mines, steel mills or garment factories, under job contracts they had signed in their distant homelands with one of the countless roving agents of the industrial expansion, searching high and low for cheap labor.

Life in America was different for these waves of immigrants, arriving as they did at a later stage in the new society's development. Moreover, they were set apart from the 'average' by their religion, education and even physical appearance. As such, the Poles and Russians, with many Jews among them, and the Italians were immediately recognizable in a community that often made little effort to conceal its contempt for those considered 'inferior'. These and other southeastern Europeans turned inward and relied more on their own group, clinging together in close-knit communities of their own. Because they differed from the 'established' American in so many respects, they had to make a joint effort to win their place in the promised land. Their growing numbers helped in this. Between 1870 and 1900, 6.5 million immigrants came from northern and western Europe, compared with about 2.2 million from southern and eastern Europe. In the following twenty

110–111. Cities flowering in the desert demonstrate how much man's ingenuity and industry can achieve. The incandescent Star Dust, one of the biggest casinos in the world, also tells us much about human nature.

years, the pattern was reversed: approximately 8.5 million came from southern and eastern Europe, against about 3 million making the journey from northern and western Europe.

THE FATE OF THE INDIANS, the descendants of the First Americans, was much grimmer. The history of relations between the whites and the Indians, in the assessment of historian Henry B. Parkes, is a sorry record of broken treaties, property violations and aggression by the white colonists on Indian soil. The unremitting pressure on the Indians continued even during the Civil War. In fact, particularly fierce battles were fought at that time against the Arapahos and the Cheyenne tribes in the Great Plains, and against the Apaches and Navajos in the southwest. When the whites failed to persuade them to move out of their traditional lands, Congress adopted a law in 1867 ordering the resettlement of all Indians in reservations. All the earlier promises to the Indians that they could keep their hunting grounds were forgotten, and even the reservations did not remain sacrosanct for long. In 1875 the United States Army, led by great veterans of the Civil War like Sherman, Sheridan and others, broke the main thrust of the Indians' resistance in the west and most of them were led off to the allotted territories in the Black Hills of South Dakota. Unfortunately, however, gold was soon discovered in the region and white prospectors and all that attended them went rushing in.

In consequence, battles with the Indians recurred, with intervals of peace, until 1890, when a new Indian policy was inaugurated. Each Indian family was allotted 160 acres of land with the possibility of gaining ownership and civil rights after a 25-year transitional period. White humanitarians, who were greatly concerned about 'civilizing' the Native Americans, instituted educational programs for the Indians and especially for their children, to eradicate their 'barbaric ways'. Land allotments not taken up by the Indians were sold on the free market and the proceeds used to finance educational programs organized and run by the Federal Indian Bureau of the Department of the Interior.

As a direct result of the federal rule on individual land ownership by the Indians, which remained in force with minor amendments until the mid-1930s, millions of acres of land that had been set aside for them actually passed quickly into the hands of whites. Over the years the Indians often sold for almost nothing the allotments they had taken. These were snapped up, especially after oil was discovered in the west. The low morale of the Indians, confined to their reservations and dependent on the government for their every need, hastened their decline. So too did alcoholism, which became a chronic problem, and probably contributed to the dwindling of the population. In the 1930s there were only about 200,000 Indians left in the United States. The right to full American citizenship of these 'sad casualties of an aggressive age' was not recognized until 1924.

SOME INDIANS PERSEVERED with their white education and acquisition of American culture and merged into the white community. Much more often, however, the tribes refused to abandon their native customs and habits, and in several cases managed to preserve their tribal organization and the mores and rituals of their ancestors. When social study and research supported the view that this was probably the best way to facilitate adjustment and socialization in the long run, the laws were altered once again to permit communal ownership of land.

This was most likely a primary factor in the resurgence of the Indian population, which had climbed to 334,000 by the early 1940s. The effects of this more sensitive policy were even more evident by 1980 when, according to the Bureau of Indian Affairs, there were about 1.5 million American Indians in the United States. Many were living in white communities at that time, but more than half were still on 279 reservations covering a total area of more than 43 million acres. However, the number of registered jobless was exceptionally high, ranging from 40 to 64 percent in the different states of the Union.

The length of time since hatchets had been buried probably played a part in the recovery of individual tribes. The Seminoles were among the last to lay down arms: they signed a formal peace treaty with the United States only in 1934, in Florida. In the Creek language 'seminole' means a runaway, for the Seminole tribe was formed by Indians and a smaller number of blacks who had escaped from slavery. They were extremely hostile to the whites. One branch of the Seminole tribe, the Miccosukee, has refused to smoke the peace pipe to this day.

The Indians still distinguish each other on the basis of tribal origin and still speak a variety of tongues and practice different customs – not all of them dance in celebration of the sun. However, today, the term 'tribe' may be used to refer to a collection of groups that speak different tongues but share a common government, or conversely, to a number of villages that share the same language but do not have a common government.

The Danes began to set sail for the New World too. A woodcut from Navigatio septentio nalis, *Jens Munk, Copenhagen, 1624.*

THE EXCEPTIONALLY DIRE POSITION OF THE BLACKS seemed inevitable from the very moment of their forced immigration. Just as historical circumstance decided the point of arrival of other groups, so it was with the blacks. But in their case it was the economic needs of others that determined their destination: the majority were concentrated in the south, where climate and soil favored specific crops and – before the introduction of mechanization – a slave-labor system. When the cotton gin brought a boom in cotton growing in the early nineteenth century, they were concentrated even more intensively in Louisiana, Georgia, Alabama and Mississippi.

Though slavery came increasingly under attack as inconsistent with and contrary to the principles of the American Revolution and the Constitution, and was regarded with loathing by many Americans, it still persisted in the southern states. Moreover, the importation of slaves continued right up to the Civil War in spite of express prohibition, for even reasonable spririts realized that in the southern states slaves were a 'regrettable necessity'. Some slave-owners appreciated the fact that the entire economy of the South rested on the slave and treated them relatively well, sometimes almost as equals. But in general there was a terrible amount of brutality, particularly on the part of white overseers on remote farms.

The Civil War was precipitated by the southern states when they opted for secession and the retention of slavery. But it was won by the North with its relatively developed industry and greater prosperity. The defeated South was compelled to agree to the Thirteenth, Fourteenth and Fifteenth Amendments to the US Constitution. These abolished slavery and made all native-born people citizens of the country with all the rights guaranteed by the Constitution, irrespective of state laws and regulations, and further, extended the right to vote to all regardless of race, color or earlier state of servitude.

But as with the liberal endeavor to resolve the status of the Indians on a basis of equality and democracy, it took a full century for the individual rights accorded by the Constitution to be affirmed and exercised in practice. Even after the defeat, the southern states could not accept the equality of former slaves. The neglected, illiterate and unqualified blacks themselves were in no position to fight for their rights and seek their 'place in the sun' along with other Americans.

The social chasm deepened between whites and blacks, the latter often being euphemistically termed 'non-whites', especially in official statistics. Antagonism frequently took the form of class conflict, particularly for whites and in small towns. The poor whites totally rejected the notion that they stood on the same rung of the social ladder as the 'slaves', and were especially incensed by the prospect of mixed marriages.

Every possible loophole and catch was exploited to subvert the blacks' new, constitutionally-guaranteed equality. Bills denying the vote to persons whose ancestors had been slaves were immediately introduced, even though they were obviously at variance with the Federal Constitution. Literacy tests for vote registration were made mandatory, or poll taxes levied, which no matter how small were still beyond the means of the poverty-stricken blacks.

ALMOST A CENTURY PASSED in this way before a special federal bill, passed in 1965, put an end to voting discrimination. When local registration clerks refused to do the job, federal clerks were sent south and registered more than a million blacks on the electoral rolls. But equality in everyday living has been a harder nut to crack and the battle is still not over. Rose Parks' unprecedented act of defiance in 1955, when she refused to give up her bus seat to a white, aroused the nation. Uprooting warped interpretations of racial 'equality' took more than government bills and persuasion. To meet the constitutional requirement of public education for all, for example, white racists opened separate schools for the blacks. It seems almost unreal today that federal troops had to be called into some southern cities just twenty years ago to enforce the ruling on desegregated schools. After desegregation in 1967, more than half a million black children were enrolled in mixed schools. The stern hand of federal power has been needed repeatedly to help erase other forms of discrimination in public life.

The blacks' experience in the north similarly shows just how thorny is the path to equality, irrespective of formal recognition of constitutional rights. There the luckier blacks inherited the unskilled jobs that had formerly been the lot of the Irish and east Europeans. Some went on to earn commendations and honors as soldiers and officers during the Second World War, and became famous in sports, films or in the theatre. But studies carried out in the 1960s showed that the blacks had lower than average income, poorer employment prospects and high rates of unemployment. Similarly, *de facto* discrimination was found to persist in respect of schooling, personal living standards and, most noticeably, in housing. The blacks had congregated principally in the abandoned and decaying inner city areas. New Harlems were springing up and with them crime and violence was on the increase. The statistics showed that unemployment was three times higher in the black than in the white population, and that most of the black unemployed were youths and the unskilled. The average income of the black household was only about half that of the white. In short, the problem of the blacks had started to boil over in the north as well. At the same time the dimensions of the problem had grown. The number of blacks in the country as a whole had soared above the 20 million mark.

THE TURBULENT DECADES began in the 1960s with the sit-ins at Greensboro, N. C. when four black students refused to leave a bar until they were served. Some 70,000 black and white demonstrators took to the streets in their support. Two years later, more than 200,000 demonstrators descended on Washington, protesting for equal rights for blacks. The black leader, Dr Martin Luther King, movingly enunciated the cause: "I have a dream that this nation will rise up and live out the true meaning of its creed. We hold these truths to be self-evident; that all men are created equal."

The Korean War had barely been consigned to memory when somewhere on the periphery of the bellicose rivalry of the two super powers, sparks began to fly over Cuba. The general mood which had begun to relax and lose some of its cold-war strains, became tense again. The United States of America next moved to intervene in Vietnam and found itself gradually embroiled in an 'unwinnable war'. Then the assassination of President John

160

The story of Pocahontas, the daughter of Powhatan, an Algonkian chief, has become a legend. She interceded and saved Captain John Smith's life when he was captured by the Indians. Later she was given in marriage to the Virginian tobacco-grower John Rolfe. But the story did not have a happy end: the peace was short-lived and the Indians were soon at war again with the pale-faced intruders.

F. Kennedy in Dallas, the bastion of right-wing southern unpredictability, at the end of 1963, sent shock waves around the world.

A few months later, tensions in the US were further heightened by the orchestrated murder of three civil rights activists in Mississippi. Part of a broad movement which included white liberals, they had been fighting for black civil rights and against the poverty and deprivation of the black population in the midst of rising prosperity and plenty. At the same time that Europe was being shaken by student riots and protests, the United States was trembling in fear of the terrorism of the Black Panthers and other extremist groups aimed at avenging all the sins committed against the blacks.

In 1968, when the war in Vietnam was at its height, America was struck by two more tragedies: the murder of the most ardent advocate of non-violence, Martin Luther King, and the assassination of Robert Kennedy. At the time when the first black woman was taking her seat in Congress, not far from the White House, and in many other cities around America, black extremists were looting and burning entire quarters, oblivious to the fact that they were undermining the concerted struggle for the rights of all citizens of the United States of America. One year later, on July 20, 1969, the American astronaut Neil A. Armstrong awed the world when he took man's first steps on the Moon. But this did not help pacify the 250,000 angry anti-war protestors that marched on Washington a few months later. President Nixon's new administration was forced to prepare the US withdrawal from Vietnam and to concentrate its energies on domestic social reforms which had been initiated more than a decade before but had been blocked by resistance rooted in centuries past.

It was a time of great turmoil in American history. Trust had to be restored in the Constitution and the fundamental precepts that had inspired the rise of the United States and the making of the nation. First and foremost, America had to make the pilgrimage to Canossa and wind up the nine-year-long 'dirty war' in Vietnam. Mustering great moral courage, the Nixon administration tried to do much more than that on the international plane – opening up to the East, and beyond that to China – in the conviction that America could not live without the rest of the world, and the rest of the world without America.

Safeguarding the constitutional rights formulated more than two centuries before was the most pressing matter in hand. Just how seriously this country takes its Constitution was plainly demonstrated when the constitutional right to impeachment was implemented, obliging Richard Nixon to resign as President of the Union in 1974.

The general attitude in those years of apathy and resignation was reflected in a survey conducted by the *US News & World Report* in April 1976, to ascertain the three most valued qualities of a national leader. Personal charisma was given the lowest rating (5.5%), and expertise in international affairs and political ability did not fare much better (15.7%). Intellectual qualities and an understanding of economics were rated higher (29.1%), common sense (52.9%) and personal courage (55.2%) much higher. However, most of all, Americans believed a national leader should have personal integrity (76.1%). In the extremely politicized atmosphere of that time, which is described by many Americans as 'tragic', the apolitical ideals of bygone generations in their quest for 'a better tomorrow' came to the fore once again.

AN ETHNIC MOSAIC

MELTING IN THE AMERICAN POT to form a new, unified American people has not quite turned out the way American visionaries and foreign travelers predicted a hundred years ago, when growing numbers of disparate ethnic groups joined the tide of immigrants. By that time, the push west and settlement of the country had been more or less completed and new-arrivals began to congregate around the thriving cities, close to ethnic or blood kin who helped them get started. Because they were scattering less, they were more resistant to the melting process. By the early 1900s American cities had become a patchwork of identifiable ethnic and racial groups straining to preserve their specific cultures and traditions in a changing, bewildering world.

The unruly cities were growing by leaps and bounds. In the fifty years following the Civil War the proportion of the population living in towns and cities climbed from one fifth to a half. Between 1860 and 1910 the population of New York grew from just over one million to almost four million; Chicago reached a population of two million; and Philadelphia a little under half a million. When they moved into the cities, and especially the smaller towns, the new American urbanites tended to retain the *laissez-faire* traditions of the countryside and set a characteristic tone of individualism. The American city was less orderly and less beautiful than its European counterpart, and seldom functioned smoothly. In fact, there was really no coherent integrated urban community, rather, the city was a collection of sub-communities.

Poor, crowded and insanitary working-class suburbs began their urban sprawl, spreading disease and lawlessness. Gangsterism, corruption and prostitution became rife. It was extremely difficult to establish and maintain a workable public order, which was moreover anathema to the adventurer out to seize opportunity, and did not suit the interests of those corrupt law-enforcers who succumbed to similar temptations.

The root problems of the cities and the organization of essential services, such as the waterworks, fire brigade, sanitary and health services and a uniformed police force, had barely begun to be tackled by the turn of this century. Here and there, urban development plans had been drawn, which usually tried, in a rather mechanical way, to avoid 'complicating things'. The city area was subdivided into squares and rectangles, blocks and streets, with little concern for aesthetic or communal needs. City regulations tended to be a hotchpotch of *ad hoc* measures to cope with issues as they came to a head. By the 1920s the cities faced a pile of chronic problems which were being multiplied by the millions of newcomers and the high birth rate.

In circumstances such as these, in the profusion of cultures and languages, the melting pot still seemed to be the simplest and most practical way of achieving some sort of amalgam. But the new pilgrims clung to their identity and turned to others of like kind. The ethnic enclave protected its members and stood behind its most successful and influential leaders. In time each chose its 'own' shops, cafés, churches, banks, newspapers and even its 'own' politicians. Ethnic lobbies and groups, especially the blacks, for example, have become a significant factor in American politics, capable of tipping the balance in a presidential or other major election. The immigrant mix of the 1920s and 1930s enhanced the importance of ethnic groups. Although there were many fewer immigrants than before, particularly during the Depression, they included a higher proportion of intellectuals and Jews from Germany and other European countries fleeing from Hitler and Stalin, as well as the imminent perils of war. They were followed out by another million people during and immediately after the Second World War.

After waning for about thirty years, immigration surged again in the 1950s, when 2.5 million people entered the United States, and continued to climb until the 1970s, when 4.5 million arrived. In the 1980s the rate settled at a level of about 550,000 a year.

All in all, from 1820 to 1985, 52,520,000 people migrated to the United States: 36.6 million from Europe, 4.6 million from Asia, and 10.5 million from elsewhere in the Americas.

THE CULTURALLY PLURALISTIC COMMUNITY that has taken shape in the United States today is more like the loosely mixed ingredients of a *salad bowl* than the compact, uniform mass in the bottom of a crucible or melting pot, in the view of the editors of the American history *A People and a Nation*. As time passed and the population grew, 'ethnic alternatives' increased, as much for the new immigrant as for the second or third generation. Although the immigrant may adopt the traditions of the *Mayflower* and learn to speak English, many still feel 'different' and under pressure to conform somehow, which is by no means easy. The US crime statistics show that antisocial conduct is higher among the children of immigrants than among children of native-born parents. This is confirmed by research in West Germany following the influx of migrant workers in the postwar period.

There is a growing trend in the United States for people to present themselves not just as 'Americans' plain and simple, but to add a label of origin – 'Irish American', 'Italian American', 'Polish American' – which is probably more than a sign of mere sentimental attachment. The very large ethnic communities that have developed are proably closely interrelated with this. Today there are more people of Irish descent in the United States than there are Irish in Ireland, more Jews than in Israel, more blacks than in many African countries. There are more Poles in Detroit alone than in most cities in Poland. Fully 400,000 Italians live in New York.

Ties with the 'old country' have become much easier with modern means of transport and telecommunications, and are obviously consolidating 'origin' as a major preoccupation in contemporary America. A certain ethnic geographical pattern is still discernible, and along with language and religion, other distinguishing features are emerging, such as age differences, for example: the average Irish or Italian American is over 30 years of age; the average American Jew, 40 years of age. The Mexican, Puerto Rican, Indian and black Americans are the youngest on average. This is partly because they produce the highest number of children, for as the song goes: 'the rich get richer, and the poor get children.'

The melting pot finally cracked under the pressures of modern times and the evolution of the concept of human rights, which, rightly or wrongly, has come to link 'equal opportunity' with ethnic origin. Now the preferred term to describe the process of making Americans, according to the *Oxford Companion to American History*, is 'cultural blending'. In his book, *Ethnic America,* however, Thomas Sowell proposes the notion of 'a complex mosaic of continually and quickly changing elements' with a clear emphasis on the

Grist windmills at East Hampton on the eastern shores of Long Island, by Harry Fenn.

omnipresent principle: everything changes. Still, the American ethnic mixture with its diversity of ancestry, languages, interests and traditions does have at least one common, omnipresent characteristic: a shared belief in the future.

THE ENORMOUS INTERNATIONAL PRESTIGE the USA had gained, and Americans' pride in it, made it especially distressing in the 1950s when the country slipped into a twenty-year-long crisis. There were many reasons for the USA's high standing: in a very short time the young country had become one of the world's greatest economic powers. The might of its arms had been proven on many battlefields before and after the Civil War, and its strategic position and war-industry potential had further grown in importance by the First and the Second World Wars.

'Tight trousers' is one way of summing up many of the problems and discomforts this vital and enterprising nation experienced in bursting out of its confines and entering the world's front ranks. It is not hard to detect the growing pains of adolescence in many of its difficulties, its indecisions, imprudence and rashness, as well as in the heaps of good intentions and lofty aspirations, which have paved many a highway to a shining future, and the occasional wrong road.

The United States entered the First World War, after much hesitation, only when it was well underway. After a year-and-a-half of fighting, in which 115,000 American soldiers gave their lives in battle, the US won recognition as one of the world's leading military and political powers. Nonetheless, in the USA there was a lingering dissatisfaction both with itself and the weight it carried in the international community. The persistent isolationists, with the considerable assistance of the Wall Steet Crash and the Depression, were soon able to tap this mood and draw the country away from the international scene again.

But the dream of splendid isolation was shattered by the Japanese attack on the American naval base at Pearl Harbor. On December 7, 1941, the United States of America was forced to take up arms again and entered the Second World War, two years after its outbreak in Europe. It stood alongside Great Britain, the USSR, China and twenty-two other countries which put their signatures to the United Nations Declaration and pledged not to conclude separate peace treaties until the enemy had been defeated.

Under the wartime regime, American industry boosted its output by 125 percent with phenomenal speed. Vast quantities of arms and material were turned out for the frontlines. By 1944 sufficient had been produced to secure victory, and industry began to switch to production aimed at the postwar recovery. With its industries booming, America's standard of living climbed quickly. Never before had Americans been so well-dressed and so well-fed. Before the war there were 50 million people employed and about four million looking for work. By 1945 a further 15 million had found jobs or were enlisted in the armed forces. There was hardly anybody that did not have an income and a decent spread on the table. New factories shooting up all over country absorbed all the manpower available. Once again, the cities began to swell.

In the course of the war effort, parallel with the unprecedented technical advances and expansion of output in industry, the United States developed and deployed the first atomic bombs, and began to explore intensively the peaceful uses of the split atom. After the war, it joined the fierce nuclear armaments race. For the Allies in Europe and Asia, victory over the Axis powers brought an end to physical danger, terror, suffering and destruction, and marked the beginning of reconstruction and recovery. For Americans, it meant a great upsurge in power and prestige, and glowing satisfaction with a job well done.

ALL THAT GLITTERS IS NOT GOLD, and nor were all these brilliant

112–113. With a lot of chuffing and snorting, train engines pulled this far-flung country together. Some, like Number 478, are still around. Now their job is to take sightseers on instructive if sentimental trips back into the not so remote past.

114. The only evidence that remains of
the gold and silver rushes are the
occasional exteriors, the rather
unprepossessing decor. In time these
vestiges could become a tourist attraction,
or the setting for an imaginative motel.

5

115.	The more fortunate mining towns of the past managed to find other options when the lucky strike ran out, and survived to become comfortable, orderly, if much less exciting places.

116.	The United States of America draws on a wide spectrum of sources to satisfy its vast appetite for energy – petroleum, coal, natural gas, water and nuclear power. But as the world's largest consumer of energy, with the highest per capita consumption, it has to search constantly for new technologies and new sources, such as solar power.

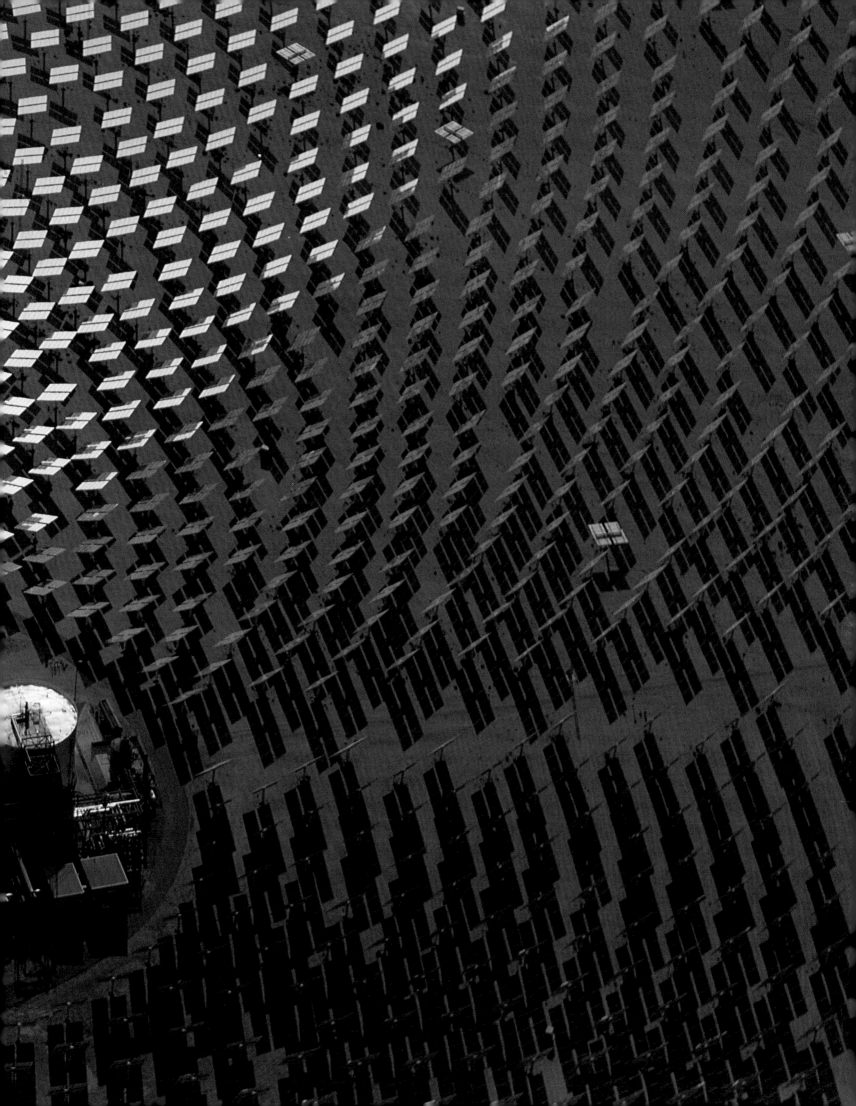

117

117.   Scientists come up daily with new ideas on how to harness, convert and store the energy of the sun. Sometimes the devices they construct look clumsy and not very convincing. But progress is rarely streamlined.

118.   Solar energy is being used increasingly in the USA. Two of the strongest arguments in its favor are that it is renewable and, above all, clean. Perhaps the cleanest of all energy sources. So clean that it positively shines!

119. Now that Man has been to the Moon, we may have to wait a long time for another equally exhilarating event – perhaps until a landing on Mars. In the meantime, the most excitement rockets will create will probably be when they go 'wandering' around on the ground.

120. The Library of Congress in Washington D. C. is one of the cornerstones of the systematic collection and storage of knowledge in the United States of America. Founded by and for Congress in 1800, it now serves as the national library and is open to the general public. It contains over 80 million items in 470 languages.

121. New knowledge and spin-off products will follow in the trail of that cosmic taxi, the space shuttle, temporarily grounded after the tragic explosion on January 26, 1986, which killed all seven astronauts on board. But the quest goes on, and by the end of this century there will probably be new feats in space.

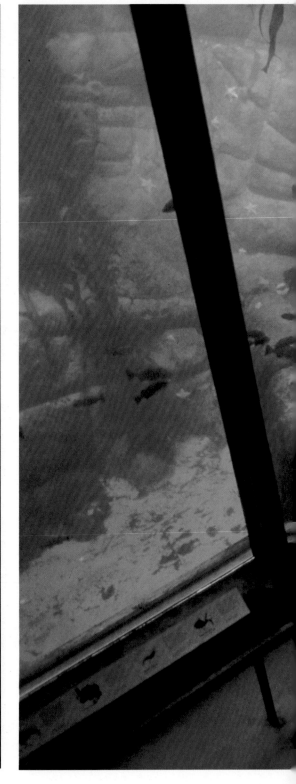

122. *The oceans and the seas are intriguing because they have kept their secrets so well for so long. Researchers have developed an impressive array of deep-sea diving equipment and underwater vessels like Professor Piccard's to plumb the depths. Curiosity has become so great and so widespread that it even pays to build great glass observation pavilions in the sea itself. At least now fish have a chance to see humans with their masks off.*

123. Nuclear fusion is being researched
intensively in the United States. Hailed as
the power source of the future, it would
harness the enormous energy generated by
fusing four light atoms of hydrogen to form
an atom of helium, the next-heavier
element. Unlike nuclear fission, which uses
the rare and dangerous uranium and
plutonium, nuclear fusion requires only
hydrogen, which is not only safe and clean
but available in abundant supply in the
world's oceans.

achievements. Victory was clouded by the postwar division of a world which was not wholly in accord with the United States' own political affinities and principles. A year before the United States plunged into the Second World War, President Franklin D. Roosevelt had proclaimed the four traditional ideals and human rights implicit in the American Constitution – freedom of speech and expression, freedom of worship, freedom from want, and freedom from fear – as 'essential human freedoms, by which a future world order could be secured'. Roosevelt had reached an agreement with Great Britain and the Soviet Union at the Yalta Conference in 1945 which demarcated separate spheres of interest, in the belief that this would promote the coexistence of the two very different political systems, the capitalist and the communist. But the postwar expansion of the Soviet Union's influence, and especially the communist victory in China, dealt heavy blows to America's confidence. In reaction to this, NATO and SEATO were consolidated at great financial and material cost, and huge sums were spent on the long war in Korea which ultimately left the image of the United States tarnished. However, by blocking the threat to Formosa, restoring Germany to the world scene as a sovereign country, and continuing to build up its conventional and nuclear strength, the United States stayed in very good form, despite the nagging doubt that it was losing ground internationally.

The four years of fighting in Europe and the Pacific gave the United States of America the moral right to a major role on the international stage, and this was reinforced *de facto* by its vast military power and unmatched economic potential. This has meant that it is always active in the front ranks – if not out front: after the French-British-Israeli war with Egypt and the withdrawal of the western countries, the United States moved into the vacuum and stayed on for several years, deepening and broadening its presence. The same has been the case elsewhere – in the Caribbean, South America, and other parts of the world, such as West Germany and West Berlin.

Standing still had never been agreeable to the dynamic Americans, and it was much less so now that they had such a high-powered economy behind them. When Khruschev made overtures, to experiment at coexistence, they were enthusiastically reciprocated – and both sides eagerly calculated their potential gains. Then the successful Soviet launch of the first man-made satellite struck the United States like a bolt of lightning and it was up and away on an all-out race to be first on the Moon.

All this may be taken as only the fair and friendly competition of *homo ludens*. But what is it that goes into the makeup of this zealous competitor? What is the American of today really like?

Campus Martius, a private fort built by settlers from Marietta, Ohio, at the end of the 18th century. Author unknown.

124. 'Eavesdropping' on space will be a valuable source of scientific data on just what is out there for many years to come. Will it also help explain the mystery of Man?

TWO CENTURIES ON

S O RAPID A CLIMB TO THE TOP was not anticipated by anyone just a hundred years ago, and few people were predicting it even at the turn of this century. History shows that a number of countries even went to war against the United States quite oblivious to the signs of its strength. And suffered defeat. Today, a clear picture of its wealth and power is continually transmitted by the media. Films and interminable television series like *General Hospital, Dallas* and *Dynasty*, along with admirable institutions like Walt Disney and his heirs, also create an image of the 'American way of life'. The clever, shrewd secret agent of the movies displaying unlimited resourcefulness in the direst of predicaments, adds a winning streak to the image. As a contemporary version of the legendary 'frontiersman', or the invincible Superman, he personifies the message that everything can change and all adversity be overcome.

Impressions gained from direct contact with the country are not quite so clearcut. Naturally, gazing down from a plane, 33,000 feet up, or through the window of a passing car or train (especially in the daytime, when flashing, multi-colored, multi-shaped signs do not magically transform the uninspiring façades) is hardly a close enough encounter to appreciate the full extent of the essential changes wrought in the past forty years, and the last two decades of breakneck expansion in particular. For this it is best to peer into the statistical records. During the 1950s and 1960s real gross national product rose by four percent or more for a full eleven years. Despite the slow down to 2.8 percent growth in the 1970s and 2.4 percent in the 1980s, it was still the highest continuous growth trend in any 'mature' economy.

Until recently, few American cities, with the exception of New York and historical cities such as Boston, New Orleans and San Francisco, could boast of a well-defined, impressive downtown or centre, partly because of the haphazard way in which they grew and partly because of the pragmatic aversion to 'unnecessary' public expense. Traveling through faceless city residential areas, alongside monster shopping malls and the innumerable sales-yards offering new cars, old cars and then new cars again, passing billboard after billboard, the overriding impression is one of empty monotony – despite splashes of flashy opulence or gaudy color, and makeshift improvisation that is not often in the best of taste. Instead, it is inside the precincts of the average family, inside the American home, with the more and more common swimming-pool, that the standard of living and the comforts of the lifestyle are best revealed. It then becomes plainer where the wealth of the USA is lavished.

The extent of the economic boom and the rise in the quality of life are indicated most clearly by the statistics on the growth of employment, output and productivity. In 1950 only 59 million people, less than 40 percent of the population, had jobs, and only 5.5 percent were registered as actively seeking employment. Despite the turbulence, social unrest, strikes and crises in the next two decades, new jobs were created at a steeply rising pace: 8 million by the start of the 1960s, another 13 million by 1970, and a massive 21 million new jobs by 1980 — almost as many new jobs in the USA as the entire populations of, say, Canada or Yugoslavia.

THE NATIONAL WEALTH GREW STRONGLY with so many hands busily at work. Yet the number of Americans seeking work kept rising, reaching 7.1 percent of the population in the early 1980s. At the same time, the new employment was not created at the expense of productivity, which continued to increase.

Despite the mild recession of 1982 and 1983, which temporarily swelled the ranks of the unemployed to more than 10 million, a total of 8 million new work-posts were created in the first half of the 1980s. The number of people employed peaked at the highest-ever level, 107.1 million, or 44.7 percent of the population, even though 7.2 percent were still looking for work. This vast labor force pushed up the gross national product (GNP) of the United States to $4,112 billion.

The significance of these figures may be gauged by comparison with other countries in the Organization for Economic Cooperation and Development (OECD). Data published in April 1987 show that all the other OECD countries together had an aggregate population of 568.8 million, or 2.3 times higher than the USA, while their total employment (229 million people) was 2.1 times higher, and their aggregate GNP only 1.19 times higher. Japan skews the OECD figures heavily and when it is excluded, the picture changes sharply: the total population of the remaining OECD countries is 1.9 times higher than that of the USA, but their aggregate GNP only 86 percent that of the USA.

The great wave of innovation that spilled out of the military laboratories into civilian manufacturing during and after the Second World War, made the USA the virtually unchallenged world industrial leader for decades. With its undamaged industry America could make anything, and because its products were the best, it could sell everything it made at home or abroad. At the same time the US was making breakthroughs in technology and production in new areas such as the application of nuclear energy, electronics and computerization, bio-engineering, robotics and the information technology revolution.

For a variety of reasons, among them the Vietnam War (and perhaps its conclusion), the OPEC oil price shocks and increased international competition, the world economy as a whole slipped into a crisis which did not bypass the USA. But its solid foundations and in particular the structure of the economy and the distribution of the work force in the different sectors of the economy, helped the US absorb the blows. Although it is one of the world's leading grain producers and exporters, in 1985 its agricultural sector engaged only 3.1 percent of the employed. This is only slightly more, for example, than the share of agriculture in the United Kingdom (2.6 percent) and Belgium (2.9 percent), which are hardly a match as far as farm output is concerned, and again appreciably less than in West Germany, France or Japan. Furthermore, US industry engaged 28 percent of the work-force, again a relatively low share compared with other industrially advanced countries, with the exceptions of Canada, Luxembourg and Australia. High productivity in industry and the strong development of the services sector in the USA explain this low share. Tertiary and other activities, the services distinctive of post-industrial society, accounted for 68.9 percent of the employed in the USA. Only Canada had a larger services sector, along with twice the proportion engaged in agriculture and a smaller share in industry.

THE RICHEST NATION IN THE WORLD is indisputably the United States of America. When national wealth is measured in terms of gross national income per capita, the tiny oil-rich countries like the Emirates and Kuwait rank highest, but excluding these, the USA had the highest gross national product per capita in the world in 1985, namely $16,773. It was followed by Canada ($15.211), Switzerland ($14,435), Sweden ($12,799), then Denmark and West Germany close together, and further down the ladder Japan ($11,863), Finland, France and the Netherlands near to par, and then the United Kingdom ($11,066).

There is, of course, a close correlation betwen average national income per capita and the level of personal expenditure and various aspects of the standard of living. One thing is clear from the outset: Americans have little compunction about spending the money they have. They were way ahead of the rest of the world in this respect in 1984, when on average they spent approximately $10,387 each. Surprisingly, the supposedly thrifty Swiss came in second, followed by Canada, France and a long way behind, West Germany and the Netherlands, Japan and the Scandinavian countries, in that order.

Americans use their greater personal wealth to buy more cars than anyone else. In 1984 there were 473 cars per 1,000 inhabitants, or almost one for every two people in the USA, as against 424 per 1,000 inhabitants one year later in West Germany, which comes second in car ownership. American fondness for television is obvious from the fact that there were 790 sets per 1,000 people in the USA, many more than in Canada (481 sets), the United Kingdom, or Australia (429). But most of all it seems they are especially attached to their radios: there were more than two radio receivers for every person in the USA in 1984, almost two times more than in Australia, the next highest in rank, and more than the UK, where there were 992 radios per 1,000 people. Contrary to expectations, the Americans did not own more telephones on average than everybody else. With 760 telephones per 1,000 it was behind Sweden's 890 per 1,000 inhabitants.

The generally high standard of living in the USA is not so well-matched by its medical services. With only 2.3 physicians per 1,000 inhabitants, the USA is behind most other industrially developed countries, such as Italy, the Soviet Union, Czechoslovakia, Germany, Spain, Hungary, etc. On another important criterion too, infant mortality, the USA compares unfavorably with fully 17 of the OECD countries. This is a very disturbing statistic for Americans, since infant mortality is considered highly indicative of the general state of health services and living conditions.

In protein consumption per capita the USA ranked third in the world. The 'latest scientific discoveries' have long been weaning Americans away from the traditional rich food. As a result consumption of meat was three percent lower, dairy products eight percent, and eggs 12 percent lower in 1980 than a decade earlier. In 1982, Americans, on average, consumed a good 104 pounds of beef, their favourite meat – far more than the next best beef-eaters, the French (68 pounds). West Germans, apparently more impervious to the bad news about cholesterol, put away 46 pounds more pork per person than Americans who, perhaps because of the attractions of the fast-food chains, hold the record for devouring chickens at a rate of 64 pounds per person, beating the Spanish (50 pounds) and the French (40 pounds). With their 200 or so different varieties of cheese, it is not difficult for the French to consume twice as much (40 pounds) as the Americans, while Swedes and Russians are more prone to indulge their sweet tooth and consume 29 pounds more sugar than the average American. Considering their low, four pounds per capita, consumption of butter and much higher intake of margarine, Americans patently know more about 'healthy nutrition' than others. Still, their consumption of only 12 pounds of fish per person makes them no match for the Russians, who ingest 40 pounds each on average. Since fish is rich in

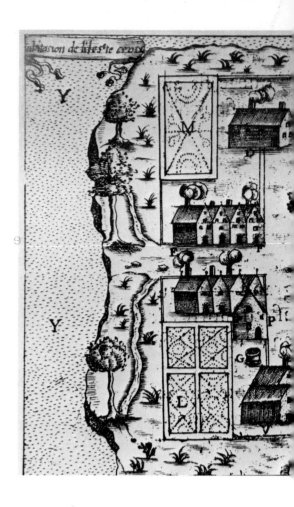

The French colony Ile Sainte-Croix (Dochet Island, Maine) was drawn by the explorer Samuel de Champlain in his Voyages, *published in Paris in 1632.*

phosphorous, which is important for brain function, perhaps one day the effects of this dietary difference on the super-power race might come up for debate.

AMERICA'S COMFORTABLE POSITION on the quality-of-life scale in the mid-1980s came with the mild recovery from the recession that had plagued all the industrial countries in the late 1970s. Industrial output in the USA was in general picking up more firmly than elsewhere, particularly after 1984. Approximately 60 percent of American families or individuals had medium to high incomes, which in official terms means that they could afford not only the basic needs – food, shelter and clothing – but the comforts of modern living. In 1982, about 12 percent of the population were living below the poverty line, drawn at an annual income level of $9,860 or less for a family of four. These families qualified for assistance from special welfare programs.

Irrespective of how often and how intensively situations resembling the 'panics' of the past and the Great Crash of 1929 may recur, certain constants will continue to be significant: the USA is one of the world's biggest producers and exporters of corn, wheat and meat, and competes with the biggest exporters of many other kinds of farm produce. Overall, the USA is the largest importer and exporter of products in the world. However, in the 1980s there was a growing deficit in its foreign trading, and by 1986 it was spending over $150 billion more than it was earning – which is one kind of cold infection that is best avoided. But then who else shall other countries sell to if not to the world's best customer, who is at the same time the world's biggest producer – and even if it is in difficulties, who could refuse to extend it credit?

The level of military expenditure is another criterion of the USA's world stature. In 1983, for example, its military outlay reached $217 billion, or the equivalent of $888 per person, and 6.6 percent of its GNP. This was some $40 billion less than the USSR's expenditure, estimated by American sources at $908 per capita, or 14 percent of its GNP. Plainly, given the world we live in and the attractions of advanced American weapons systems, military alliances with the USA will continue to be a major feature in its international relations and trade. For countries that, at particular junctures in their history and for reasons best known to themselves, are ready to use 29 percent of their GNP for military expenditure like Israel, or 24.3 percent like Saudi Arabia ($2,508 per capita), or 47.2 percent like Iraq ($787 per capita) in 1983, obviously the sums of money in question are of less importance than the deliveries.

GET RICH QUICK, QUICKER, QUICKEST, along with the maxim 'Time is Money', has been one of the basic mottos of the USA. 'Fast' and 'instant' in a million variations for every need and circumstance are the products of the ethos of a perpetual race and the motivating forces of renewed dynamism. The 'fast', 'speedy', 'swift', 'instant', 'special', 'express' services that beckon the American from all sides constantly reinforce and deepen the feeling that everything is in some process of becoming, happening, that everything must be done in a hurry, the goal or destination achieved as quickly as possible.

The food industry plunged into this perennial race early on with a tasty selection of ready-made meals, seconded by the cooler industry which has equipped every US householder with 1.4 refrigerators and deep freezers. Thousands of restaurants and cafeterias in a multitude of chains offer dishes with carefully measured proteins and calories, served in various shapes and forms, hygienically and attractively packed, and at reasonable prices made possible by standardized mass production. This still leaves room, however, for old favorites like milkshakes and slices of 'mother's own' pie. The history of McDonalds, which opened its first outlet in 1953 and was serving 46 million meals a day by 1986, indicates that fast food is more than just a cheap, easy substitute for the Mediterranean morning snack or the full-scale lunch requiring a siesta for proper digestion. It has taken on a revolutionary life of its own as a civilized, standardized, sterilized, virtually automated operation that reduces to a minimum possible the time it takes to 'tank up' without overloading the stomach or leaving a litter of dishes and pans for someone to clear. But in the USA even a cup of coffee is not stretched out into a ritual of measured sips and relaxing gossip or worldly debate, oblivious to the passage of 'wasted time'.

The American mania for time-saving practicality has spawned a new breed of 'drive-in' services of numerous and often astonishing kinds. The proliferation of the automobile, with almost one car for every two people, including children, has made a profound impact on the lifestyle of the American, who tends to wear his car like the astronaut his space suit. When he is encapsulated in his wheeled container there is less need to be finicky about dress, particularly the lower, invisible part. Ensconced in the car, little Americans do the shopping with their parents, drive through 'safari' and national parks or drive-in aquariums, snuggle down to sleep on the back seat after a drive-in hamburger while their moms and dads take in the drive-in movie. In time they park their own cars to watch the wonders of the sunset, or sunrise, and smooch before heading for the drive-in bank to take out an 'instant' loan by phone, and are soon taking their offspring to a drive-in church, until the time comes to bid farewell in a drive-in funeral home.

Statisticians in the USA keep records on just about everything: from aspirins, lipstick and disposable diapers, to 'participation in outdoor recreation activities', meaning how many people spend how much time jogging or running, bird-watching or off-road vehicle driving, picnicking, or just walking for pleasure. In his sampling of facts, *In One Day,* Tom Parker worked out that Americans made 800 million telephone calls a day in 1984, more than the equivalent of fifteen centuries of one-minute conversations. The long-distance phone bill for America that statistical day came to $120.6 million, or $84,000 a minute. As if that were not expense enough, they spent over $14 million on lottery tickets, and gave away $165 million the same day. They also wrote half a million letters to Congress and 20,000 letters to the President, while 200 of their compatriots just did not have the time because they became millionaires, and 110 lucky golfers were making a hole-in-one and did not really care.

Measuring, recording and keeping score is a great American pastime, and of course every statistic is potentially interesting for the market, for business, as well as public administration. The greatest attention is paid, understandably, to those who have succeeded, in anything whatsoever, for in principle everything can be turned into business.

THE MOST OUTSTANDING PEOPLE in the USA are usually, although not exclusively, considered to be those who are the most successful, and in turn these are defined as those who earn the most, in line with the Protestant work ethic and under the irresistible influence of the media. There are precise inventories of the number of 'wealth-holders' with gross assets of $300,000 or more, and the number of millionaires. In 1982 there were more than 4,377,900 people in the first category, making up a little under two percent of the population, and 407,700 millionaires. Whether the small number of millionaires has anything to do with the platitude that 'good people are rare' remains to be seen. It has been established, on the other hand, that both the wealthy and the millionaires are concentrated in the south, and that they amassed their fortunes mostly in the west.

Ownership of company shares is another dimension of the way of life, at least for some Americans. Most shareholders are urbanites: fully half of them live in cities with over a million inhabitants. Although their total number rose from 30.8 million in 1970 to 42.4 million in 1983, it fluctuates quite considerably, particularly in response to recessions or the prospect of recessions: in 1975 it dropped to 25.3 million, but climbed back up to 30.2 million in 1980 as 'confidence' gingerly improved. The decline in the early 1970s was evident in the cities, but was more marked in the non-metropolitan areas, which were also slower to rebound when faith in the stock market revived. In terms of age, the most avid share-buying cohort is the group between 21 and 34 years, and in terms of education, the group who have attended university, which tends to tie share ownership in with the higher income brackets. In 1983, more than half of all shareholders had an annual income of over $25,000. As a rule, the higher the annual income the more constant the shareholder, whose deeper pocket obviously helps allay market anxieties in times of an economic downturn. Geographically, shareholders tend to gravitate to the south and west, but the statistics do not indicate whether this is because the Sun Belt allows more time to read the very fine print of the stock exchange reports by the harsh light of day, or just because these are the sort of people who prefer to loll in the sun.

The south and west of the United States of America have been attracting a lot of people over recent years in strong migratory flows that have rapidly swelled the population of these states. In the 1970s Florida, for example, recorded a 43.4 percent population growth, Nevada 63 percent, Arizona 53 percent and Wyoming 41.6 percent. In part the figures are high because of the low base population, but then strong growth was also evident in Texas (27 percent) and California (18.5 percent). On an average day in 1984, according to Tom Parker's *In One Day*, as many as 1,287 people migrated to California. With the exception of Anchorage in Alaska, which experienced a 30 percent increase in population in the early 1980s alone, the Sun Belt is by far and away the most magnetic region of the USA. In just four years, from 1980 to 1984, the population of as many as ten out of the eleven big metropolitan areas in Texas and Florida jumped by at least 20 percent. By 1984, the USA as a whole had 37 cities with a million or more inhabitants.

Americans have always been mobile as part of their still fresh migrant heritage, but this propensity to move is becoming more rather than less pronounced. At the beginning of this century the majority of families who moved at all did so at most once or twice in their lifetime, and usually only within the confines of the same country or state. In the 1960s as many as 18 percent of the population were moving house every year. Later, in the 1975–80 period, 45 percent of the 48 million families in the US resettled at least once.

Just over half of them moved 'down the road' to another part of the same county, about 20 percent moved elsewhere in the same state, and almost as many crossed statelines. The principal reasons for pulling up stakes were job-related and reflected shifts in regional economy, such as the decline of the textile industry in the northeast or coal mining in Virginia, the growth of the automobile industry in Michigan, the phenomenal rise of the aviation and space industries, electronics and the film industry in California. In the same period, 1.4 million people quit the northeast and 1.2 million the north central regions, while the south and west received millions of newcomers. Several million Americans are poised to set off in any direction at any time in their four million trailer-homes.

As it turns out, Americans have been taking the old pioneering prescription 'Go West, Young Man', very much to heart all along. In 1980 the census reconfirmed that the 'center of population' of the United States, the population gravity center, is creeping steadily westward. The western leanings of the American people were first detected in the Second Census taken in 1800. The center of population is the point at which the USA would balance if it were a weightless rigid plane and the population were distributed on it with each individual person being of equal weight and exercising an influence on the central point proportional to his distance from it. At the first census in 1790, the population gravity center was at 39016'N and 76011'W – or 23 miles east of Baltimore in the state of Maryland. At the 1980 census it was about one degree further south and more than 14 degrees further west – 3808'N and 90032'W – or roughly a quarter of a mile west of Desoto in Missouri. If this trend persists, by about the 600th anniversary of the Constitution the population center will be at Los Angeles, and unless a lot of man-made islands have been built in the Pacific by then, a lot of Americans will be very wet! Although at some point, west of west should become east, which may confuse the pilgrims.

The following engravings and woodcuts, 'the work of eminent American artists', are 'a delineation of the mountains, rivers, lakes, forests, waterfalls, shores, canyons, valleys, cities and other picturesque features of our country'. They date from the fifties, sixties and seventies of the past century, and appeared in Picturesque America, *an excellent two-volume work marking the first centennial of the U.S.A., edited by William Cullen Bryan and published by D. Appleton and Company, New York.*

Spears Wharf in Baltimore, by Granville Perkins (1830–1895).

125. Livestock farming is much more than just a profitable occupation that has helped to make both the farmer and the nation wealthy. It was long ago elevated to the rank of a special craft bordering on art. Indeed, it has had an impact on all the arts in the United States, beginning with folk songs.

129

126–127. Vital ingredients in the burgeoning of livestock farming were the invention of barbed wire to keep cattle and sheep from overrunning farmland; the windmill to pump subsurface water; the railroads; the invention of cans and the refrigerator; and of course the indispensable cowboy with his amazing lasso.

128. The US livestock industry has its distant origins in the millions of native buffalo, which the pale-faced pioneers well-nigh exterminated, and the thousands of cattle running wild in the West which are assumed to have descended from a mere six cows and one bull that the Spanish shipped into Mexico in 1521.

129–130. The tales of the ranchers, their clashes with the Indians over possession of the land, their struggles against the elements, and their fights with each other, have been a major source of inspiration in American literature.
The melancholy ballads of the cowboy were composed around lonely camp-fires at the end of a hard day in the saddle, and sung partly to calm the tired and nervous cattle: a far cry from the rock scene.

131

131–132. Nutrition standards in the United States are among the highest in the world. However, in recent years meat consumption has been declining, largely because of fears about cholesterol levels and excessive protein intake. But health concerns and good resolutions go only so far: annual beef consumption is still about 80 pounds per capita, although pork consumption has dropped below 60 pounds. Needless to say, farmers try to keep track of health trends and fads, and to predict market demand.

133

133. *Farming household incomes are, on average, lower than those of industrial workers, but the healthy outdoor life and satisfaction afforded by the work are compensation enough for many farmers.*

134.   *A recent development in US livestock farming is the rise in horse breeding, as more people take up horse-riding and go to horse races. The huge race prizes are a big incentive to owners, breeders and jockeys alike. Besides, there is the indisputable fact that horses are just more elegant than other farm animals.*

135.   The great majority of farmers are
very traditional in their tastes. For them
there are no greater events than the
livestock shows, their farmers' association
meetings, and the rodeos with contests of
skill and courage that have been popular for
generations.

136.   No matter how painful the
experiences of others, advice falls on deaf
ears when some passion gets under the
skin. A fall, far from discouraging, is one
reason more for trying again to master and
subdue.

138

137–139. *All eyes are on the arena. Thousands of hands involuntarily reach out to grasp the reins, pull them tight, loosen them, pull aside, dodge, and wait for the right moment to gain the advantage. And then it all starts again, over and over. In the show business era, the ancient trial is transformed into a carefully conducted ritual.*

140

140. *What satisfaction when resistance is broken and the animal tamed! The two former adversaries are joined in a single, synchronized action that is dictated by the victor.*

141. Nostalgia for the pioneering days of the Old West makes the waggon race a popular event.

142. Not unlike the astronaut in training for a space flight, the novice rodeo rider has to go through simulation training that tries to foresee every conceivable eventuality. But the simulation computer is not all-knowing yet – all least that is what the second-timers claim.

143–145. The United States is still the world's leading exporter of agricultural produce, although its farm population has been shrinking steadily. In the mid-eighties, a mere 2.2 percent or just one in every 45 Americans was engaged in agriculture.

146. Everything the United States of America has accomplished ultimately stems from its highly-productive agriculture: its relatively few farmers bring in high yields largely because of the extensive and innovative use of mechanization and technology in a society which places no limitations on farm size.

147. Many farmers are quitting now because of declining incomes. In the mid-eighties, for example, the average farming family was earning only three-quarters as much as the average family outside agriculture. Even so, new tracts of land are steadily being brought under cultivation and the process of turning America into a blooming garden continues apace.

148. America's high farm production has made it the source of half the world's exports of corn and sorghum, three-quarters of the soybean, a quarter of the wheat, almost a fifth of the tobacco, a sixth of the rice, and a tenth of the cotton traded on world markets.

ENJOYING LIFE

WHAT THE AVERAGE AMERICAN SPENDS HIS MONEY ON is one clue to what he does when he is 'doing nothing'. All leisure time activities involve more or less personal or family expense which – though far less than the costs of basic needs – still amounts to vast sums of money for the 'leisure business'. In 1985 American personal (or family) consumption expenditure reached the astronomical sum of more than $2.6 trillion, and 6.7 percent of this, or about $176.3 billion, was spent on 'recreation'. However much other things in the USA may change, statistics show that there has been very little alteration in the pattern of personal consumption over the past ten years, just as personal habits tend to be rather resistant to change. The slight shifts, even of a percentage point or two, may give a hint of the directions which change might be taking.

Food, drinks and tobacco account for about 20 percent of the family's or the individual's personal consumption (21.3 percent in 1980 and 19.3 percent in 1985). Clothes, footwear and personal effects like toiletries, watches and jewelry absorbed a further 9 percent or so of the household budget. Housing expenditure took roughly as much as the first two groups together – about 30 percent, with about 15 percent going on rent or own-home costs, and the remainder on home operation (utilities, furnishings, appliances, telephone, domestic service, etc.) and transient (hotel and other) accommodation.

Medical expenses, another major item in the budget, include health insurance, which encompasses about 66 percent of the population, medical and dental bills, drugs and hospital expenses: the costs of serious or long-lasting illness can bring a family to the verge of bankruptcy unless it is well-covered by insurance schemes. In 1980, 10 percent and five years later 12.5 percent of personal expenditure came under this heading. In 1981 the average American spent $975 on health care and the average family of four $3,900.

Travel is one of the bigger family budget items, making up about 13.5 percent of total personal consumption expenditures. In the American house-hold local and long-distance public transport costs are minor in comparison with the much more common 'user-operated travel', that is, the costs of private transport. Given the relatively thin networks of local public transport systems, the private automobile is no status symbol (although the model of the car is another matter) but a basic necessity in many instances, which may in part explain the teeming 126.7 million automobiles on the roads in 1983.

'Personal business' expenditures – for legal services, brokerage charges, investment counseling, bank service charges, safe deposit box rentals, and finally funeral expenses – accounted for 6.8 percent of total personal consumption. College and private education fees consumed only 1.6 percent ($41.9 billion), somewhat less than religious and welfare activities, which accounted for a little over two percent in 1985 ($56.1 billion). Foreign

149. Despite modern technology, good harvests still depend a great deal on the weather. When the need arises, the whole family turns out to get the work done in time. Continual improvements in farm equipment are reducing costs and labor input, and raising the quality of production.

travel, it is curious to note, accounted for only a little over a half of one percent of total consumption, or $ 13.8 billion.

WHAT AMERICANS DO FOR RECREATION was the subject of a Gallup survey in 1984. It was found that about 40 million Americans (47 percent of all adults) like to grow flowers in the garden, 40 percent spend part of their leisure time vegetable gardening, and 41 percent swimming, 33 percent bicycling, 30 percent fishing, between 23 and 20 percent go camping, jogging, bowling and/or do aerobics, while 19 to 10 percent spend time weightlifting, playing billiards or pool, and playing ball-games like volleyball, basketball, baseball, golf, tennis or table tennis, motor boating, canoeing and rowing. Less popular sports, or those engaged in by less than 10 percent of adults, include roller skating, horseback riding, target shooting, skiing, water-skiing, sailing and touch fotball. All of these leisure-time activities account for less than two percent of recreation expenditures.

Although as a share of total consumption expenditures outlays for recreation did not change from 1970 to 1984, the sums of money involved climbed from $ 41.3 billion to $ 157.1 billion in that period of time. Besides purchases of flowers, seeds and potted plants by the green fingered, tickets to spectator amusements and sports events, pleasure aircraft and other, smaller sports equipment, this sum also includes the cost of books, newspapers and magazines, musical instruments, radios, television sets and video recorders and their repairs, cinema, concert and theater tickets, and holiday travel. There was a slight decline in the relative outlay for books, newspapers and magazines in this period, which may be connected to the larger sums spent on phonograph records and magnetic tapes, imports of which multiplied ten times over.

NEWSPAPERS, MAGAZINES AND BOOKS have long been fixtures in the life of Americans. In 1984, a total of $ 19.5 billion was spent on them, or about 12 percent of all the Americans' recreation expenditures. Despite the four percent drop in the relative share of these outlays since 1970, any suspicions that people in the USA are watching television and listening to the radio more than they are reading and playing instruments, must be tempered by the fact that actually more and more books and sheet music, at decreasing prices, are being sold each year.

Before Independence there was little to boast of by way of literary accomplishments in the 'New World', but newspaper publishing got off to an early start with the first issue of the Bostonian *Newsletter* in 1704. In 1741 Bradford's *American Magazine* and Franklin's *General Magazine* came out. From the beginning, the press was valued highly as an independent commercial operation, while its special role in society was expressly recognized by the First Amendment to the US Constitution.

The first American play, *Prince of Parthia,* was written by versatile, self-taught Thomas Godfrey in 1767, and the first novel, *Power of Sympathy* by William H. Brown, in 1789, but the American Revolution did not inspire great works. Ralph Waldo Emerson, one of the 'ideologues' of Puritanism and the belief that each individual represents a part of the Divine and hence must be acknowledged to have goodness, called for a break with 'Europe and the dead cultures' and exploration instead of 'our own world'. But little of lasting value came out of this.

With their American themes, Ralph Waldo Emerson, Walt Whitman and Henry David Thoreau stand out in the nineteenth century for their optimistic treatment of the situation of the individual: man was considered a rational being in the image of his Creator and was therefore fundamentally good. Edgar Allen Poe, Nathaniel Hawthorne and Herman Melville, in contrast to this romantic view of the individual, were concerned with human misfortune, unconvinced of the goodness of the individual or society's ability to reform. In addition to the poems of John Greenleaf Whittier and the stories of Harriet Beecher Stowe, who wrote much of merit in addition to *Uncle Tom's Cabin*, outstanding works were those by Emerson, with his vast self-assurance and egoism which served the interests of the times; Hawthorne's *The Scarlet Letter* with its refined and sceptical artistic reflections, unquestionably the first American novel of high standard; the poetry and stories of Edgar Allen Poe, the American exponent of *'l'art pour l'art'*, whom Baudelaire admired immensely and popularized in Europe; and Herman Melville's *Moby Dick*, the tale of the pursuit of a white whale, the symbol of evil against which man struggles in vain.

The prolific New York writers included eminent authors such as Washington Irving and James Fenimore Cooper, whose five-volume novel *Leatherstocking Tales* about the hunter and scout, Natty Bumpo, cast the mold for the courageous but modest, self-confident but woman-shy, historical inhabitant of frontiersland.

But none of these 'founders' of the American literary tradition could compare with the formidable Mrs Eden Southworth, whose sixty or so novels were published before the turn of this century in runs of 100,000 copies, thanks to the cylinder and rotary printing presses that had revolutionized printing in the mid-nineteenth century.

A CRAZE FOR READING NOVELS, especially low-cost editions, soon took root once these presses started rolling and turning out runs of up to 50,000 copies. It all began with the forerunners of the modern paperback: the Sunday supplements to the daily newspapers. These took advantage of the lack of copyright protection for foreign authors and pirated major British authors such as Charles Dickens, Walter Scott and many others. Their mass production approach to the press, the written word and the media in general, in which the market was the final arbiter of accomplishment, led to continual technological and editorial innovations which have steadily improved productivity and lowered prices.

These technological innovations were also a major factor in the development of 'personal journalism' by powerful and not uncommonly eccentric individuals who started up the first modern-style newspapers like the *Tribune, Times, Sun* and *Herald*, particularly in New York, before and after the Civil War. They originated organized news-gathering by a network of reporters and correspondents using the telegraph and other fast-relay methods of communication, and gave increasing space to commercial advertising, inaugurating the trend to commercialization that predominates today. The history-making events of the era firmly established the papers, whose concise, plain language was tailored as much to those always pressed for time as to immigrants struggling with English.

The cataclysmic transformation of American life brought about by the Civil War did not inspire any masterful literary works. Then, in the 1880s, Mark Twain and Henry James arrived on the scene. The recognition of copyright for foreign authors toward the end of the century focussed attention on domestic writers, who had previously been too expensive. This encouraged the rise of the American realists and naturalists, such as Stephen Crane, Frank Norris, Theodore Dreiser and Willa Cather. The first decades of the twentieth century brought a welter of works by David Graham Philips, Upton Sinclair and Jack London. But these and later writers of literary distinction — Sherwood Anderson, F. Scott Fitzgerald, Ernest Hemingway, John Dos Passos, Thomas Wolfe, William Faulkner, John Steinbeck, and later Henry Miller and contemporary masters such as John Updike, Normal Mailer, Philip Roth, Eudora Welty and Bernard Malamud — are for the most part not as widely read as the ever-growing hordes of 'lightweight' writers. Best-sellers like *Anthony Adverse* by Allen Hervey and *Gone with the Wind* by Margaret

Mitchell in the 1930s set higher reader standards, but it is still hard to imagine anything to compete with the print runs of detective stories or their impact on the printing industry.

Eight native-born or naturalized Americans have been awarded the Nobel Prize for Literature: Sinclair Lewis, Eugene O'Neill, Pearl S. Buck, William Faulkner, Ernest Hemingway, John Steinbeck, Saul Bellow and Isaac Bashevis Singer.

In colonial America, many were tempted by poetry-writing, largely in the English style. Philippe Freneau (1770s) is considered the first real American poet, but literary historians generally skip the names of the early bards and their flowing, waking-dream poetry without cognitive content or close connection with real life. William Cullen Bryant made his mark with *Thanatopsis* at the beginning of th nineteenth century, and Walt Whitman's *Leaves of Grass* (1855), although aesthetically incomplete, was significant for the formation of American national awareness. Poets bridging the period between Whitman and the twentieth century include Emily Dickinson in the first place and, of lesser stature, Sidney Lenier and William Vaughan Moody. Edwin Arlington Robinson won acclaim with his lyrical narrative poems as one of America's great poets in the years between the two world wars. The leading mid-century poets – Robert Frost, William Carlos Williams, Marianne Moore and Robert Lowell – have been succeeded by a new generation: John Ashbery, Allen Ginsburg, Galway Minnell, W. S. Merwin, Gary Snyder, Adrienne Rich and James Merrill.

THE MEDIA BOOMED IN THE 1980s. More than 9,000 newspapers are now being published, 1,700 of them dailies with a combined circulation of 62 million. Large sections are given over to commercial information and advertisements, so that as a rule they are voluminous. The Sunday papers, which have circulations totalling some 56 million more than the other dailies, sometimes weigh more than two pounds. Over 11,300 different periodicals are published, about 7,000 of them as weeklies. The American news magazines, with their synthesized news reporting and analytical commentaries, such as *Time, Newsweek, US News and World Report* and *Business Week*, have set a worldwide trend and won mammoth circulations. But the greatest readership has been captured by the *Reader's Digest* and the *TV Guide*, which have circulations of 17–18 million, with the *National Geographic* coming a close third.

Book printing has also been growing by leaps and bounds: in 1970 a total of 36,071 titles were published, and in 1984, 51,058. Technological developments in printing have steadily reduced costs and spurred this great surge. In 1984, 1.5 billion copies of paperbacks were sold, and a further 768 million hardcover books, when multi-volume editions like encyclopedias are counted as a single title. Each day a million books are sold in the USA in a wide variety of ways and places. About half are sold in general stores and bookshops, a tenth in schools, a twentieth through the mail, and a solid quarter from paperback bookstands scattered at every turn.

Relaxing with a book is cheaper for the 10 million and more Americans who belong to the numerous book clubs and circles and regularly receive copies, selected from the 47,000 new titles published each year, at reduced prices. But it is cheaper still when there is a library at hand. American readers take out more than 500 million books each year. There are over 32,000 libraries in the country, more than a third of them free public libraries. Institutions of higher education house nearly 5,000 libraries, the largest of which is the Harvard University Library. However, the Library of Congress in Washington, which was founded as a specialized congressional facility in 1800 and now serves as the national library, storing a copy of every book published in the USA, is the largest in the country.

With his Indian allies from the Algonkian, Huron and Montagnais tribes, Champlain defeated the Iroquois in 1609.

The Book Industry Study Group estimates that in 1983, 57 percent of women and 42 percent of men in the USA read at least one book every six months. The most avid readers are young adults from 16 to 29 years of age, generally from the better-educated and higher-income (over $40,000 pa) bracket. Six percent of the population read nothing at all, neither books, periodicals nor newspapers.

RADIO, TELEVISION AND FILM have all made an enormous impact on contemporary America and been given strong impetus by its great technological flexibility as well as its dynamic economy. Radio began its sweep across the nation in the 1920s. Today there are nearly 10,000 radio stations broadcasting entertainment programs and airing news and information in an unending stream that keeps listeners up-to-the-minute, and whets their appetite for other media – newspapers, television, books and the arts. The sheer number of radio receivers – approximately 2.7 for every person in the country – assures that Americans are 'tuned in' at all times and in all places. Precisely because of its all-pervasiveness, US sociologists credit the radio with playing a crucial role in the homogenization of the urban and rural parts of the country.

Cinematography, one of the great phenomena of the twentieth century, made its American debut with the 10-minute film story, *The Great Train Robbery*, directed and shot by Edwin S. Porter in 1903. Charlie Chaplin, Mary Pickford, Douglas Fairbanks and William S. Hart were the great stars of the silent movies made in Hollywood, on the outskirts of Los Angeles, which was soon established as the film capital of the world, thanks to its abundant sunshine and variety of natural settings. The first sound film, *The Jazz Singer*, starring Al Jolson, ushered in a new era in which the cinema rapidly overshadowed the theater. The 2,000 or so stock theater companies operating throughout the USA at the beginning of the century were reduced to a quarter of the number by the 1930s. More recently, however, theater groups have begun to enjoy a strong revival.

Despite the great popularity of radio and television, the motion picture remains the American public's great favorite. More than 200 large and small film companies supply the market with films for a variety of purposes, from educational to advertising to entertainment. At the start of the 1980s there were about 16,000 motion picture theaters and some 2,800 drive-in movies where great numbers of Americans spend their leisure time and their money; almost as much was spent on movie theater admissions as for all drama, concert and sports events combined in 1983. And no wonder. The film studios churn out vast numbers of films. Box-office hits like *ET the Extra-terrestrial*, *Rambo*, *Star Wars*, *Return of the Jedi*, and *Back to the Future*, attract huge audiences and generate enormous profits.

A demand for high-quality films has been fostered by the expansion of television, which in 1986 was supplying non-stop entertainment on the 121 million television screens located in 98 percent of American homes. Viewers do not pay a penny to watch programs on most of the 900 commercial and over 300 public television stations, which enlist advertisers and sponsors to bear the costs. The enormous sums spent on television productions directly or indirectly help support numerous sports clubs and functions, as well as theaters and music and ballet ensembles, which have recently begun to win the assistance of various government and other public and private foundations. The advent of cable television has added a new dimension to the viewing menu. For a subscription to the 100 or so cable television companies, viewers can take their pick of light entertainment or sophisticated educational, scientific or current-affairs programs.

Information processing and data services linked to television sets or home computers are opening up undreamed of vistas in the development of the media.

CONCERT AND THEATER ATTENDANCE is becoming more and more popular in America. Measured in terms of personal expenditure, they still account for only about a quarter of the money spent on amusements, spectator sports and movies, but in 1984 that still came to more than $2 billion.

The growing interest in the performing arts is tied to the development and rise of 'American music', which until the twentieth century did not amount to more than 'music in America'. Classical or 'serious' composers closely followed European models and trends and centered their work on hymns and ecclesiastical music. It was only toward the end of the last century that Edward MacDowell broke new ground with musical compositions imbued with an 'American spirt' – native Indian themes and rhythms. The movement this engendered led to an interest in black music as well; the Czech composer Antonin Dvorzak incorporated negro melodies into compositions such as the *New World Symphony* after a visit to America. In the 1920s and 1930s George Gershwin, composer of *Rhapsody in Blue* and *Porgy and Bess*, drew brilliantly on the Afro-American musical heritage. Simultaneously, a third well-spring of 'original' American music began to gush to the surface – the songs and ballads of the pioneers of the American West.

American jazz conquered its homeland and then the rest of the world. The development and spread of radio and recording techniques, and excellent vocalists and instrumentalists – Bing Crosby, Louis Armstrong, Benny Goodman, Judy Garland, Frank Sinatra, Glenn Miller, Elvis Presley, Bob Dylan and innumerable others – have carried American popular music to all parts of the globe, and opened the way for the huge, pulsating US show business.

At the same time, ground-breaking experiments by American composers with atonal music and advanced atonal systems have brought many illustrious names in the world of serious music to the USA. Numerous distinguished composers have emerged, among them Aaron Copland, Virgil Thomson, Roger Sessions, John Cage and Leonard Bernstein. Other important contemporary composers include Milton Babbitt, William Schuman, Gian-Carlo Menotti, Elliot Carter, Ulysses Kay, Gunther Schuller, David Del Tradici, Philip Glass and Steve Reich. Their appearance is doubtless closely related to the growing number of symphony orchestras around the country. Over the past hundred years 1,572 have been established in the USA. The Boston, Philadelphia, New York, Chicago, Minnesota and Washington symphony orchestras are renowned worldwide. Nearly 20 million people attend orchestral concerts a year. The most famous events are the summer festivals in Tanglewood, Massachusetts, and Aspen, Colorado.

The story of opera in the USA is very similar. For many years there was a great dearth of opera, which the Metropolitan Opera Company in New York made up for to some extent during the season by Saturday radio broadcasts of its performances throughout America. Interest in opera has grown fairly quickly in recent decades: there are now 133 opera companies in the country.

The American speciality which attracts the largest audiences is without doubt the 'musical' or musical play which combines song and dance with stories of dramatic interest. The musical, usually a lavish spectacle, is launched on Broadway, the showcase of American theater, and if successful goes 'on the road' around the country and beyond. The big hits are almost invariably made into film versions, and may run on Broadway several years. Some of the most successful since the war have been *Oklahoma, Fiddler on the Roof, Hello Dolly, My Fair Lady* and more recently, *Hair*. The absolute record-holders for number of performances are *Grease* with 3,388, the revised version of *Oh Calcutta!* with 4,283 and *A Chorus Line* with 4,536 performances by July 1, 1986.

Fifty or more plays open each season on Broadway, still the drama center of the USA, although 'regional' theater has been developing over the past thirty years with the support of a widening circle of patrons and subscribers. The repertory of plays by established authors like Eugene O'Neill, Tennessee Williams, William Saroyan, Arthur Miller, and Edward Albee is constantly expanded by new authors. There are about 20,000 non-professional theater groups in operation and some 70 new theaters have been opened.

Ballet, both traditional and modern, has enjoyed a similar growth in popularity. The best known companies are the New York City Ballet, the American Ballet Theater, the Alvin Ailey Dance Company, the Joffrey Ballet, the Dance Theater of Harlem and the San Francisco Ballet. Outstanding choreographers like Jerome Robbins, George Balanchine, Martha Graham, Paul Taylor, Merce Cunningham and Eliot Feld, and celebrated dancers like Suzanne Farrell, Mikhail Baryshnikov, Judith Jamison, Fernando Bujones, Gelsey Kirkland and Allegra Kent have helped to raise the standard of American ballet to the highest level.

THE GENERAL FLOWERING OF ART AND CULTURE in the USA has been both symbolized and assisted by the foundation of two of the country's greatest arts centers. The Lincoln Center in New York justifiably lays claim to being the 'greatest performing arts combine in the world'. It encompasses the Metropolitan Opera Company, the New York Philharmonic, the Julliard School of Music, a repertory theater and a library museum. The other is the John F. Kennedy Center for the Performing Arts in Washington D.C., which has three stages for opera, ballet, drama and music and also includes the American Film Institute, the National Symphony Orchestra, the Washington Opera and the American National Theater.

These and many other landmark public buildings of various kinds have greatly enhanced the image of American architecture in recent decades. Authentic American creations employing original designs and visions of a post-industrial future are making inroads amid the welter of historical architectural styles, the chaotic confusion of the aesthetic and the functional, the pretentiousness of the bloated neo-classicism, ugly railway stations and public utilities. The ranks of the giants of American architecture: Buckminster Fuller, Edward Durrell Stone, Frank Lloyd Wright, Ero Saarinen, are being joined by contemporary masters of innovative design such as I. M. Pei, Philip Johnson, Charles Moore, Kevin Roche, Michael Graves, Robert Venturi and Richard Meier. Architects have found scope for their talents and often for innovation in the building of art galleries: the Metropolitan Museum, the Museum of Modern Art and the Guggenheim Museum in New York, the National Gallery and the Hirshorn in Washington, the Art Institute in Chicago, and the Museum of Fine Arts in Boston.

Over 100 million people visit painting and sculpture exhibitions every year and, thanks to the rich patrons of bygone times, become acquainted with the artists and styles of the past as well as comtemporary American art. Before, and for decades after the American Revolution, puritanical sternness and sobriety, and the mediocrity of the newly-rich, did little to foster artistic talents. In contrast to Mexican and South American art, Indian traditions were totally ignored in North America except in the Spanish southwest, where they fused with the Spanish-Mexican style. While architecture, especially in Washington, adopted the dignified Federal style, thanks largely to Thomas Jefferson, who was awed by the architecture of Rome, painting and sculpture were long preoccupied with portraying dignitaries and worthy citizens or glorifying historical events in the Colonial style (John Vanderlyn, John

Trumbull and Washington Allston). More interesting works of art were produced by the less ambitious landscape and genre artists (Thomas Cole, William Mount, George Caitlin and Henry Lewis) who recorded scenes of Indian life.

Gradually people of money and influence gained an appreciation of European art, not to mention the commercial potential of the fine arts in general. After the Metropolitan Museum was opened in New York in 1870 and galleries began to appear in other cities, public interest and the numbers of artists notably increased. Impressionism exerted a strong influence: the most gifted and versatile artist of that period was John La Farge. Many painters traveled abroad: Mary Cassatt worked in France, and John McNeill Whistler and John Singer Sargent in England. Outstanding works from those years are the interiors of the Boston Library and the Library of Congress, the Capitol, and Trinity Church in Boston.

At the end of the nineteenth century two groups emerged: one that depicted real life 'as it is', led by Robert Henry, and another more sophisticated school led by the artist-photographer Alfred Stieglitz. The former group made its mark in history largely through 'The Eight' exhibition in 1908. The naturalism of this school earned its disciples epithets like 'Apostles of Ugliness' and the 'Ashcan School'. Steiglitz's school experimented with form and approached cubism, fauvism, futurism and dada-ism. Both schools exerted a powerful influence on subsequent developments in US art. The sensational Armory Show riveted world attention on American art, and a new impetus came when the Museum of Modern Art in New York and various foundations began to build up their collections. The US Government began to patronize the arts for the first time during the New Deal. With the WPA art project in 1935–40, about 5,000 artists were engaged in public programs, providing mosaics and murals for public buildings. This not only ensured a living for many, but also heightened general interest in the arts. A peculiarity of those times was the gaping difference in the salaries: while male

English cod fishermen curing and drying their catch in Newfoundland. Drawing by H. Moll, London, 1720.

150–151. *Ninety-one percent of the population growth in the United States of America in the early eighties was concentrated in the South and the West of the country. The population in these parts grew by 11 million in those five years. The metropolitan statistical area of Dallas-Fort Worth reached 3.5 million people and surpassed Washington D. C. The Houston-Galveston-Brazoria metropolitan statistical area, with 4 million inhabitants, climbed to eighth place in the nation.*

153

153. *Something is steadily emptying out the states of West Virginia, Pennsylvania, North Dakota, Oklahoma and Wyoming. Maybe it is the sunshine enticing people to the South and the West. Maybe it has something to do with the fading of old Civil War prejudices. Or with well-directed economic promotion programs.*

Illustrated: the city of St Louis on the Mississippi River.

152. 154. *One reason for the growing trend of migration to the South and West may well be the pleasant, comfortable lifestyle fashioned by southern tastes with their interweave of black culture.*

Illustrated: streets in New Orleans, famous for its jazz and its old French quarter.

painters were paid on average $1,150, females earned as little as $500 a month.

Prominent modern painters include Georgia O'Keefe, Robert Rauschenberg, Jasper Johns, William de Kooning, Helen Frankenthaler, Frank Stella, Robert Motherwell, Andy Warhol and Andrew Wyeth, and a younger group – Julian Schnabel, David Salle and Robert Longo, to mention but a few. Eminent among the sculptors are Alexander Calder and David Smith, Louise Nevelson, George Segal, Isamu Noguchi, Mark de Suvero and Robert Irwin. Pop art, op art, abstract expressionism and environmental art placed America in the vanguard of world art in the mid-twentieth century.

THE GREATEST FUN AND THRILLS for many an American are to be had out on the playing-fields. The huge interest and wide participation in sport in the USA is one of the outstanding phenomena of this century. The end of the Civil War (1865) signaled the advent of sports as they are known today. The early settlers did not have time for 'sports' and most of the competitive fun centered on work-related chores like bee-husking, log-rolling and turkey shoots, although chances to indulge in a little betting were not lacking, given the boxing matches, cockfights and horse races. But it was not until the industrial revolution started amassing people in towns and cities that spectator sports first became really popular. Boxing and baseball were two of the earliest of the big-time draw-cards, later joined by American-style football and then basketball. The great American boom in active, amateur, participant sports came after the Second World War with increased wealth, a higher standard of living and more free time.

Almost everybody in the USA, irrespective of age or walk of life, seems to be into some sort of sport, whether recreational or competitive. Organized sport starts in the earliest school grades and by the time the teenage level is reached the competition is in earnest. The traditional egalitarian openness of competition in US sport, combined with the lure of lucrative 'play for pay' professional contracts, and the national fame that envelops stars, all encourage wide and intense participation in sports. The achievements of American sportsmen and women are well-known. They dominated the track and field events at the very first modern Olympics in 1896, and American athletes have brought home more gold medals than the sportsmen of any other nation. At the 23rd Summer Olympics in Los Angeles they carried off 174 medals – 83 gold, 61 silver and 30 bronze.

Since the war, professional and amateur sports together have become one of America's biggest industries. Intercollegiate sport is an outstanding feature. Although strictly speaking amateur, it generates huge profits, involves multi-million dollar budgets and has a devoted following of millions of fans. The major schools compete with each other in football, baseball, athletics and other events in what has become a high-stakes business and promoter of an excellent network of sports facilities: stadiums, arenas, training camps and the like. The athletes, non-professional at this level, receive free tuition and living expenses, and the enticing prospect of climbing the ladder to top-paying professional status. Glamorized by the media as national heroes, like the legendary Babe Ruth, superstars in US sport now command more attention and salary than the president.

TRIPS ABROAD ARE MORE AND MORE COMMON items on the leisure agenda, but Americans still spend by far the greatest part of their free time at their clubs and various other organizations related to sports interests, hobbies, religion, ethnic group or nationality, business, patriotism, cultural or charity activities. At an early age they start by joining the Boy or Girl Scouts, school or local clubs. As an adult the American male likes to socialize in business, professional or fraternity organizations like the Elk, Lions, Rotary and Moose Clubs, some of which still have a color-bar – for whites only.

155.   Who could fail to feel at ease and yield to the pleasures of languor here. Even the tireless Mississippi begins to loaf when it reaches these parts at the end of its 2,348-mile journey.

Women's clubs are frequently work-related – for nurses, secretaries and the like, and are usually rather small in size. All-in-all, clubs and societies of these kinds occupy more of the average American's time than even sports.

A trip to one of the 48 national parks in the USA rates as the all-round favorite pastime of the American family. Each year they are visited by 42 million people, who also have another 31,000 parks and recreation areas to wander through, enjoying such scenic attractions as Niagara Falls, the Grand Canyon and Yellowstone, and the many historical sites, as well as man-made delights like the Disneylands near Los Angeles and in Florida.

However, judging by how many passports are taken out, which is an indicative, although not exact measure, Americans have been developing a great taste for globe-trotting: in 1970, some two million or so passports were issued, and in 1984 more than double that figure. Whereas before foreign travel mainly lured the young, the itch has spread more evenly through all age groups in recent years. Europe and the Mediterranean are still the main goals of a good half of all American travelers, who, however, are individually spending less time and much more money abroad. In 1970, 5.2 million Americans traveled abroad on average for 27 days, spending $18.15 a day, or an estimated $4 billion in all (trips abroad include travel to neighboring Mexico and Canada). Fourteen years later, in 1984, the figures had altered substantially, with 12 million traveling for an average of only 17 days at a cost of $51.88 per day, and leaving behind $16 billion.

It is curious that a good fifth of these modern explorers are over 60 years of age. Foreign travel apparently comes on the agenda for those who have 'done their share' and are free from pressing cares like looking after the family, schooling the kids, or paying the house mortgage. Considering that in 1984 more women than men applied for passports, it could almost be concluded that women have fewer cares, or at least one less.

An Indian family preparing chemuck in Yosemite (Great Grizzly Bear) Valley in the Californian Sierra Nevadas. Drawing by James D. Smillie.

WHERE NEXT?

THE PROBLEM OF THE MAN ON THE BICYCLE remains, at least theoretically, in spite of all the impressive and not infrequently astounding facts and figures on the USA. It is not at all clear how it should be solved. Luigi Barzini stated the problem elegantly in *Harper's Magazine,* in 1981:

''These multiform people are united mainly by their resolute, beaver-like determination to construct a more rational and just society, possibly one day a perfect society, which of course, like the cathedrals of old, may never be completed. The dream of the future is important. The United States has been compared to a man on a bicycle, who will collapse if he stops pedaling and moving ahead.''

Besides its advanced technology, seemingly cheap energy, and bountiful agriculture, which indeed is not as economic as it sounds, the picture of America has been drawn to a great extent by all those Americans ecstatically burning-out at work. The top jobs, which usually have the highest salaries, are held by the kind of people who come to work early, stay late into the evening, and then take work home with them — much easier now that computer terminals are made to suit the color schemes of the marital bedrooms. The type of people, in other words, who would probably become ill if they had no work to do.

Europeans picked out certain of the distinctive traits of the American back at the beginning of the last century: when voicing admiration for him, they usually gave the Protestant work ethic as an explanation; but some of them barely concealed a certain epicurean disdain.

''In Europe people talk a great deal of the wilds of America, but the Americans themselves never think about them; they are insensible to the wonders of inanimate nature and they may be said not to perceive the mighty forests that surround them till they fall beneath the hatchet. Their eyes are fixed upon another sight: the American people views its own march across these wilds, draining swamps, turning the courses of rivers, peopling solitudes, and subduing nature. This magnificent image of themselves does not meet the gaze of the Americans at intervals only; it may be said to haunt every one of them in his least as well as in his most important actions and to be always flitting before his mind. Nothing conceivable is so petty, so insipid, so crowded with paltry interests — in one word, so anti-poetic — as the life of a man in the United States.''

Alexis de Tocqueville, the peregrine French liberal politician and writer that Americans are so fond of quoting about themselves, wrote this in his *Democracy in America,* in 1835. The modern American — at least up to 1980 — seems to be just as haunted by this same 'magnificent image' and 'view [of his] own march'. In a Gallup survey conducted for the American Chamber of Commerce that year, 'doing the job as well as possible' was important to 88 percent of the respondents, who were all employed and obviously ready to push the pedals full steam. The Protestant work ethic which sees work as a way of serving God has evolved in modern days into the view of work as a cultural value, and is obviously all-pervasive in America even at the beginning of the third century of Independence. The sociologists Daniel Yankelovich and John Immerwahr found proof of this in a study carried out for the Public Agenda Foundation: more than half of the respondents reported that they have 'an inner need to work as well as possible, regardless of pay'. But they also found that 62 percent of those interviewed believed that 'people do not work as much today as they did five or ten years ago'.

Regardless of whether this is correct or not, can Americans afford to stop pedaling so hard and so fast? In the early 1960s industrious Americans were producing a whole nine-tenths of the world output of color television sets. However, by the mid-1980s it had become plain that there were 'workaholics' elsewhere, especially in Japan and other parts of Asia, just like those that created the American wonder. Japan was already making half of those television sets and nine-tenths of the world's video recorders. Moreover, it was beginning to take the lead in that traditional American domain – automobile manufacturing. In the last decade of this century, the USA, which once made almost half the world's automobiles, seems likely to import about 40 percent of its cars. Similarly, the US share in world machine-tool exports had slipped from 23 percent in the mid-1960s to about four percent by the 200th anniversary of the Constitution.

One hundred and fifty years after de Tocqueville's perceptive explorations, the average American is required to work only 40 hours a week. The rest of his time is free. Has he changed? Is he, for example, more poetic?

BENEATH THE APPARENT CONTINUITY created by loyalty to the 200-year-old fundamental principles of the USA and their constant invocation, a great deal has altered of course. In place of a nation of three million people, largely of British descent, a veritable ethnic mosaic is spread across the continent. On January 1, 1986, there were 239.4 million Americans. Demographers estimate that the black population grew 6.7 percent a year after the 1980 census and reached a total of 28.6 million in 1986. The white population grew at only about half the pace (3.2 percent) and numbered approximately 201.4 million in 1984. The blacks' share of the population rose slightly from 11.8 to 12.1 percent. Spanish-Americans have become a major ethnic grouping that makes up 6.4 percent of the population and is growing at a faster-than-average rate: Hispanic families average 3.89 members compared with 3.22 for other families.

The backlash of the baby-boom generation, which was reaching mid-life in the 1980s, is the aging of the US population. The average age in 1971 was 27.9 and in 1984 31.2 years. Further, the contingent of school-age children (5–17 years) began to shrink after 1980 in 40 states as well as in Washington D.C. The sharpest population drops were in the national capital (15 percent) and Massachusetts and Connecticut (13 percent). Experts, such as Richard Easterlin of North Carolina State University, theorize that the baby-boomers faced fiercer competition for jobs and then promotion, had greater difficulties in founding homes and families, and consequently had fewer children. But these fewer children will have proportionaly more of their own, Easterlin suggests. This trend may already be perceptible: in 1984 there were 17.8 million live births, the highest birth rate since 1968. On Easterlin's theory of self-initiating demographic-economic cycles, the 'shrunken' generation will produce a bigger one, which in turn will experience the characteristic higher rate of illegitimate births, divorce, stress, crime, suicide and social and political alienation. But the question is whether or not other factors will intervene to constrain population growth.

Captain John Smith became Admiral of New England, which he reached in April 1614. This map, drawn two years later, was well known to the Pilgrims; they preserved the names Plymouth, Cape Anne, and Charles River.

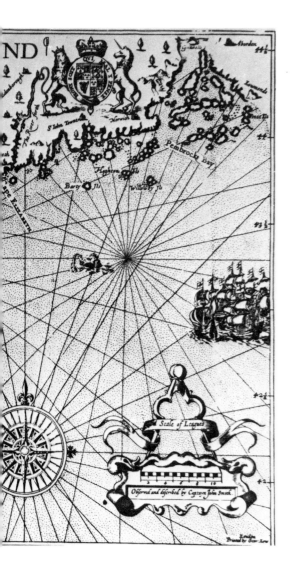

Capitalist economies, and the USA's among them, undergo periodic undulations. The best-known are the so-called business cycles which, according to some interpretations, last three to five years, while inventories build up. When inventories become excessive a crisis erupts, orders are cut back, production declines, workers are laid off, and inventories eventually reduced until business revives again. US economist Simon Kuznets also identified 20-year economic cycles related to cyclic changes in capital investment, rather than inventories. Although there are many analogues in the US history of 'panics' and depressions and the Kuznets theory has yet to be fully proven, the baby-boom of the postwar periods fits into Kuznets' description rather well. *Chi vivra, vedra* – who lives, shall see!

THE FLOURISHING EARLY 1980s brought a faster rise in the number of US households, which grew at a rate of eight percent and reached a total of 86.8 million, in contrast to the population itself which increased only 5.7 percent. At the same time people were marrying later – men at an average age of 25.5 and women at 23.3 years of age in 1985. In recent decades there has been a rise in single-person and non-related multiple households. Family households made up a little over 70 per cent of the total in 1984, but only approximately four-fifths of these included both parents. Single-parent families were five times more frequently headed by a woman than a man; these women were black eight times more often than white; and under 35 years of age in almost 40 percent of cases. The number of female householders has gone up steadily from one decade to the next.

There were 87.8 million men in the USA in 1985, some eight million fewer than the number of women. More men than women never marry, while there are more single divorced women than men: in 1984, there were 7.4 million divorced women and 2.5 million fewer divorced men – who usually turn right around and get married again, or soon die. This may also be seen from the ratio of widows to widowers – 11 million to 2 million, or 5.3 to 1 in favor of widows. With such a wide field, older men rush into marriage. In 1979 for example, 37,118 men and 21,762 women over 65 years of age got married, of whom 853 of the brides and as many as 1,726 of the bridegrooms were marrying for the first time.

A gender difference is also evident in regard to the 20 million single-person households in the USA that year, for 62.3 percent of these solitary dwellers were female. Over 95 percent of children under 18 years of age were living with their mother, with or without their father. Of the 50 million married couples in the USA in 1984, 762,000 were racially mixed black and white, and a further 587,000 in other racial combinations, with considerably more whites of both sexes involved than blacks.

THE GREAT CRISIS IN THE AMERICAN FAMILY is as much a topic of discussion as in other advanced countries, and possibly more so considering the more intensive research in the USA. Without pretending to an analysis of the causes, it is relevant to note the growth of female employment. The ratio of employed men to women changed substantially in just the first four years of the 1980s – from roughly 62 to 38 in 1980, to 59 to 41 in 1984. This trend reflects the rising level of education as well as the greater involvement of the woman outside the family, the ramification of the sexual revolution and advances in birth control. Together these factors can run directly counter to the traditional ideas of the family and the shared hearth. Some statistics are indicative here.

The number of married and divorced Americans 18 or more years old would suggest that enthusiasm for wedlock is waning. From 1980 to 1984, just four short years, the number of married men declined from 76.4 to 65.8 percent, and the number of married women from 71.6 to 60.8 percent. While for white men and women the percentages were slightly above the average levels, they were noticeably lower for black men and women and showed a stronger decline of 18 percent for men and 22 percent for women. Related to this, there was a rise in the percentage of divorced people: a two percent rise for men and a 5.4 percent rise for women on average. Black women showed the biggest rise – from 4.8 to 11 percent.

In 1980 there were 2.4 million marriages and 1.1 million divorces registered in the USA, or on average 490 divorces for 1,000 marriages. The highest divorce rate in regional terms was recorded in Arkansas (864 per 1,000 marriages), Oregon (775), Arizona (659) and Florida (646). The most critical years of marriage, when divorces occur most often, are the first six. Statistically, after this the risk of divorce declines steadily so that after thirty years of marriage it is very low. At that point, presumably, the spouses are just grateful to be alive.

The age of spouses and their maturity and tolerance are a factor in divorce. The most critical age for divorce is between 25 and 29 years. Women who divorce before 30 years of age usually opt for a second try and more than three-quarters of them remarry. For those over 30 at the time of divorce, the frequency of remarriage declines with the years rather markedly. Those in their 30s remarried in 56.2 percent of cases, those in their 40s in 32.4 percent of cases, and women in their 50s in only 11.5 percent of cases. Curiously, the corresponding chances for men to marry again have not been studied in such detail.

A solid two-fifths of all divorced women take the plunge at least once more. But having children tends to lower the likelihood, even though the reverse would probably be preferable for the family *per se*. Again, the younger the divorced mother, and the fewer children she has, the higher the frequency of remarriage. Divorced men tend to remarry more often than women – 78.3 percent of them. The problem is that men do not live as long as women on average. In the USA there are only 88 men per 100 women in the 55–64 year age group and fewer than 67 per 100 in the over–65 group. This explains why more divorced men remarry than women – they simply have greater opportunity. Often they try to turn back the clock and marry women younger than their first wives, which might be one explanation for their relatively earlier deaths!

FAMILY PLANNING AND BIRTH CONTROL are becoming established features of the American way of life. In 1982 over 36 percent of the 54 million women of child-bearing age in the USA were using contraceptives: about 40 percent of married women, a third of the unmarried and about the same percentage of formerly married women. That same year eleven out of twelve white women said they wanted their child at the time of conception, or almost then, but only three out of four black women did.

In addition to research into the number of wanted and unwanted births, of married, divorced or unmarried mothers, the use of this or that kind of family planning, recourse to abortion and the like, detailed studies have also been carried out into the sexual behavior of American women. In 1982, 57 percent of white and 80 percent of black women had sexual relation before marriage, 17 percent and 27 percent respectively by the time they were 15 years of age, 50 percent and 76 percent by the time they were 18, and 63 percent and 80 percent by the time they reached 19. There is no need for comment on dearth of comparative data for men.

Even in absolute terms, the majority of unmarried mothers are black, although the number of white women bearing children out of wedlock increased in the early 1980s. In 1984, for example, 355,000 more unmarried white women gave birth, whereas the figure for black women was only 5,000 higher.

The great sexual liberation of recent decades has resulted in more frequent births out of wedlock among the youngest groups. In more than 80 percent of cases the 15–17-year-old mother conceived her child, and in 57 percent of cases gave birth out of wedlock. These figures decline sharply with age: in the 20–24 year age group only a quarter and in the 25–29 year group only a tenth of mothers conceived before marriage. Three-quarters of the unmarried mothers that gave birth in 1982 were under 25 years of age, with just as many in the 15–19 as in the 20–24 year age group. About 57 percent of black and about 12 percent of white women that gave birth were unmarried. Fully a fifth of all births that year were to unmarried mothers.

In any case, the welter of statistical data collected in the USA on very personal matters says a great deal about the statistical 'culture' of American citizens. They appear to be either inured to constant badgering about what they did/did not, would do/think/like/dislike, or profoundly aware of the benefits of such close study of behavior for the individual as well as the nation. But, no matter how much the 'traditional' family is in crisis, surveys show that the great majority of Americans still believe it to be the basic unit of American culture and civilization, and that it must be renewed through better education, more family planning, and above all, improvements in the economic status of those social groups or classes in which it is most jeopardized. The aftermath of divorce, particularly in families with children, not only leaves marks on those directly involved, but affects society at large.

ALTHOUGH ALL AMERICANS ARE BORN EQUAL, this statement refers of course to equality of opportunity in principle. When life warps this fine rule and people find themselves without enough food, clothing or adequate housing, no job or income, or an income that is too low, help is needed. Although the United States of America is the wealthiest country in the world, there have always been some people in the clutches of poverty who go hungry, even in times of great prosperity. Poverty is precisely defined in the USA as the lack of the 'means to obtain an amount of food, a standard of living accommodation and other goods that seem adequate to a particular society'. The difficulty is that all the measurements involved have to be made in terms of monetary income. The American government has been attempting this

'Warping' or hauling a steamer through a whirlpool on the Tennessee River, by Harry Fenn (1838–1911).

each year since it began to undertake systematic care of the needy in the 1960s. In 1984, 33.7 million incomes were officially classified as below the poverty line.

The causes of poverty in the USA differ widely: large families, an unskilled head of family who works full-time but earns too little, long spells of unemployement, business venture failures – and there are 20,000 of these a year – and especially the big drop in income at retirement, which ranges from 20–50 percent. Experts estimate that retirement incomes or pensions should be at least 60–70 percent of income just prior to retirement, with regular adjustment for rising living costs. But this kind of goal is unattainable. It is estimated that one sixth of the over-65 population in the USA now lives below the poverty line. This is an improvement over 1970, when the figure was estimated at fully a quarter. Economist Thomas C. Borzilieri calculates that millions of older Americans may be considerably worse off than the statistics show but are just not poor enough to qualify for support.

Clearly the assessments are relative. Nominally, the US poverty line income would be quite agreeable to half the worker families in western Europe and certainly many more in eastern Europe. Even the poor American family is not expected to do without a radio, refrigerator and television set. Some find it hard to be without an old car, and they prefer to scrimp on food and clothing. Nevertheless, the number of Americans below the official poverty line is too great, particularly when it is considered that almost a third of the black population and 28 percent of the Hispanics and other non-whites fall into this category. The sheer proportions indicate the extent of the social problems involved and the potential confrontations, or at least the diminished social motivation and the alienation. Apart from the 6.7 percent of upper-class households with an income of over $50,000 per annum, in 1985 only a third of all US households achieved a standard they considered 'comfortable', let alone approximating the 'American dream'.

The pretty little village of Red Bank below the Neversink Highlands, by Granville Perkins.

156–159. Nothing can hold back America's migratory flocks on their way to sunny California. On the other side of the forbidding desert lies the fertile soil of the Pacific coast, where millions from the East find new homes.
The nation's population center has been shifting steadily westwards. Since the 1980 census, it has moved to about 10 miles northwest of Potosi in west-central Washington county.
Today it takes just a few days for a trainload of fresh peaches, apricots, grapes, almonds, avocados and olives to cover the distance which the first settlers needed five months to cross.

160

160–161. The leader of the first group of pioneers to reach the West Coast wrote: ". . . to our great delight we beheld a great valley, very fertile, and the young tender grass covered it like a field of wheat in May." Little has changed since to deter newcomers.
Glenway Wescott described the West Coast valleys in his book The Grandmothers: *"They came to the Far West and found valleys as large as kingdoms, without kings . . ."*

162

163

162–163.   Not far from shores of the Pacific, as one guide book lilts, "stretch gentle valleys, a prosperous region of family farms, towns, orchards and fields which are green all year..."

164

164.	Once the trail to the lush Pacific coast
was blazed, the groundwork was laid for
the creation of a continental nation.
From the beginning, the Pacific coast's
great attraction was the abundance of food
it proffered. For a time, however, the
settlers valued furs and skins much more
than the perishable salmon, which they had
no way of stocking.

165.   The seaside is especially attractive
for leisure time. The climate allows year-
round frolicking in and near the water and
time unbounded to invent new sports and `
activities.

166

166. The population of the San Francisco–Oakland–San Jose agglomeration, or metropolitan statistical area as the technical jargon goes, reached more than 5.8 million in 1985. In just five years it increased by almost 450,000, making this metropolitan area the fourth largest in the nation, displacing the Philadelphia–Washington–Trenton area on the other side of the continent.
Illustrated: a space-age cathedral in California.

168

167–168. San Francisco probably gained more than any other place from the City Beautiful movement launched by architect Daniel Burham at the beginning of this century. The movement stressed the importance of civic centers, parks, boulevards and transportation systems to make cities more attractive, as well as economically efficient. The Golden Gate Bridge and famous streetcars have become San Francisco's trade marks.
The city's great influx of American migrants must certainly be attributed in part to its magnetic and glamorous aura. But another important factor is that San Francisco has the highest per capita income of all the 100 biggest cities in the United States. In the mid-eighties it reached 20,000 dollars.

169–170. *Chinatown in San Francisco is truly a city of its own. Here China is not so far away, even though newcomers from the other shores of the Pacific have added a distinctive flavor.*
Nothing is missing, not Chinese inscrutability, nor Chinese dragons, nor the typical Chinese eating parlor, at least as it is imagined by those who have never been to China.

171–172. *Chinese feel very much at home here, though instead of jogging for miles they tend to prefer traditional forms of exercise. To keep fit, of course, in the best American tradition.*

172

173

173.   *The highways that interlinked the separate towns of past years have become the arteries of vast megapolises. Along with Bowash on the East Coast, the region of uninterrupted urban settlement lying between Boston and Washington, or Chipitts stretching from Chicago to Pittsburg, on the West Coast there is now San-San, encompassing San Francisco, San Diego and everything in between.*

174.   The climate and laid-back atmosphere
inevitably breed lifestyles that diverge to
a greater or lesser extent from those
adopted in more demanding climes or
times. The relatively higher divorce rate in
the West is one indicator of the dilemmas
that arise.
Illustrated: a ''Hollywood'' mural.

174

177

175–176. The high standard of living can often blur the dividing line between reality and fantasy. Like the strange wall paintings and the reflections in the glass façade.

177. Sensations are multiplied by the magical city lights. Bathed in variegated bands of color, even the bystander becomes a participant in a moving work of art, a happening.

178.   In San Francisco's Haight Ashbury
district, the hippie Hashbury communal-
living experiment was launched by the
'flower children' of the sixties, inspiring
many to emulate them or try something
new in their search for an alternative
lifestyle, and themselves.

179

179–180. *Illusion is the essence of the Hollywood 'dream factory', which continues to fascinate, titillate, horrify and amuse film-fans the world over.*

180

181

183

181–182. The coming years will bring further changes and innovations in this dynamic society. There will certainly be material progress, and fewer unfortunates will be stifled by poverty. Many will try to avoid the pitfalls that previous generations could not escape as they strove for success. All in all, the American dream will persist. More will fulfill their dream than ever before, but as always, it will depend on them.

183. Success in the highly-competitive US society often entails taking chances as well as seizing your chance. Film-making is certainly a risky business, for studio head and stuntman alike.

THE A PRIORI EQUAL CHANCE FOR EVERYBODY remains the main motive for pursuing the American dream, which is no less beautiful today than it has been imagined by Americans and many others since the time the Supreme Law of the USA was first written.

In truth, today about half of all property in the USA is held by just one-tenth of the population. Although in Great Britain, for example, fewer people own even a greater share of the property, the distribution of net income is less equitable in the USA than in the UK or other western European countries. Yet this is fully in accordance with the American conception of equality, which in practice means equality of opportunity for everyone to acquire wealth by his own efforts, freely and with a minimum of government or other social impositions, but gives no guarantees.

Neither aristocratic titles nor hereditary privileges have ever been granted in America. A survey conducted by the *Scientific American* illustrates how far this ensures equality. In a representative sample of 1,000 people, approximately a quarter said they came from poor, and a tenth from rich families. The majority of them, including 10 percent or so from working-class families, reported they had the opportunity to continue their schooling at university. Those from wealthy families were generally able to enroll in the best colleges, and they did enjoy certain advantages in getting good jobs quickly, though perhaps not quite as good nor as quickly as the televisual

The South West Pass in the delta of the Mississippi, by Alfred R. Waud.

184. Marilyn Monroe, a part of the American dream.

scions of *Dynasty* in Denver, Colorado. But it was found that diplomas or family connections are of little help later on in life unless the person proves his own worth in practice.

In the USA no special privileges accrue from particular church, ethnic or regional membership. The rules of the market apply to everyone equally, although of course this does not mean that the USA is entirely free of injustice. On the contrary, many forms of discrimination plainly still exist. Only a few years ago many whites as well as numerous blacks thought *nothing* would ever change regarding civil rights for blacks in the South, and it seemed that prejudices against the Poles, Italians or Jews would *never* be erased. But in the past twenty years or so there have been great advances in these respects.

People will always try to gain a certain edge, an exclusiveness on the basis of sex, ethnicity or membership of one of the 338,244 churches, attended by a total of 140 million Americans. It is safe to conclude that for at least some time to come there will be a tendency for blacks to cluster together in inner city areas and whites to congregate according to ethnic or cultural sensitivities. Accents and idioms will go on being a mark of differentiation in the same way as when Bernard Shaw saw the common language 'English' as dividing the Americans from the British.

The breadth and level of education in the USA is a major corrective that will assume increasing weight in the future. The number of people with tertiary education has been growing especially quickly over recent decades, particularly in the black population. From 1965 to 1980, for example, the number of white university students rose 66.9 percent and the number of black students 267.5 percent. In the 1940s only one-quarter of all American males over 25 years of age had finished high school, and less than four percent had completed a four-year college course. In 1980, these figures had climbed to 66.3 percent and 16.3 percent respectively. Furthermore, in 1980, 45.7 percent of the seven-million-strong army of Americans who had a college degree went on to graduate studies.

With their 'culture of speed' Americans have been adjusting rapidly to the changes taking place in science and technology. Well-informed and attuned to the needs of the market, the labor force has been undergoing a revolution of its own. Among the 950,000 students graduating with bachelor's degrees from colleges or universities in 1980, which was 19 percent more than the number just a decade before, there were 58 percent fewer graduates in mathematics, 45 percent fewer in language and literature, 32 percent fewer in social sciences, 26 percent fewer in teaching and 11 percent fewer music and art graduates, than in 1970. By contrast, there were about 25 percent more graduates in psychology and the biological sciences, 55–79 percent in economics and technology, and particularly big increases in architecture and agriculture (133–152 percent), medical (more than twice as many) and computer science graduates (six times as many).

So much else has changed too. The whole world is living in a time of extremely rapid, extraordinary change on the economic and the political front – in the balance of power and relations between states. In 1950, the USA accounted for 52 percent of the world's gross product, Henry Kissinger noted at an Aspen Institute for Humanistic Studies conference in Berlin late 1987. ''At that time'', he said, ''we did not have to worry about the balance of power because we were the balance of power; the fundamental American foreign policy problem at that time was to identify a difficulty and overwhelm it with resources. Today the United States represents maybe 20 to 23 percent of the world's gross production. It is still the largest single economic unit in the world, but it is confronted with a totally different set of foreign policy challenges.''

At home too the changes have been tumultuous. Many taboos have been lifted, many false idols have fallen, and many a high-sounding phrase has been reduced to a laughing-stock. In their place new values are being created. New institutions are emerging and the roles of established ones changing, breaking up the monopolies of the earlier order. Information at the speed of light is altering the US and the world economy. Because of its experience with a continental economy, the USA is perhaps "uniquely situated to lead the world into a new era of economic cooperation", as President Ronald Reagan claimed at the start of 1988.

YET THERE IS STILL THE CYCLIST — with an ever shorter working week but nevertheless flagging drive. How can he stay the fastest in the saddle, preserve his way of life, and still turn out two and three times more than others? He could stop his bicycle and get off, and switch to a new vehicle, to new technologies of the twenty-first century. Or start turning the wheels of a new industrial and social revolution. Or he could find an entirely different motive for pedaling so hard, one that transcends the pay packet and the consumer goods it represents. Motives more like the sense for free-wheeling action and innovation that leads Americans to open half-a-million new businesses each year, putting everything at stake.

In any case, the inveterate American pioneers and adventurers in constant quest of new territories have reached a new frontier, a new installment of the Great American Dream.

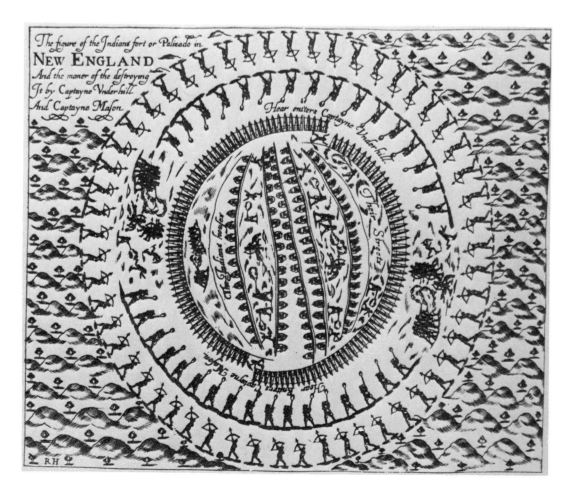

The figure of the Indian fort or Palizado in New England

MEMORABLE DATES IN US HISTORY

1492
Christopher Columbus and the crew of the "Santa Maria" discover the Bahamas on October 12.

1497–1540
John Cabot, exploring the northeast coast, reaches Delaware. Giovanni de Verrazano enters New York Bay after an expedition along the New England coast. Juan Ponce de Leon explores the Florida coast. Hernando de Soto lands in Florida and crosses the Mississippi. Spanish explorers reach the Rio Grande, Colorado River, Grand Canyon and Californian coast.

1565–1609
Pedro Menendez founds St Augustine in Florida. Captain John Smith founds Jamestown, the first permanent English settlement in the New World. Exploring the Northwest Passage, Henry Hudson sails from New York Bay into the interior.

1620
The pilgrims from Plymouth land on December 21, after three months of sailing in the "Mayflower". Their Mayflower Compact will serve as a basis for government and have an impact on subsequent laws and general principles.

1636
Foundation of Harvard College at Boston.

1664
British take the province of New Holland and the city of New Amsterdam; both renamed New York.

1756
Start of French and Indian Seven Years' War.

1763
French lose Canada and the American Midwest.

1763–1775
Escalating conflict between the colonists and Britain, with growing resistance to dependence, taxes and the like, culminates in military confrontation. George Washington is appointed commander-in-chief and seeks an alliance with France.

1776–1783
Declaration of Independence, July 4, 1776. Battles of the Revolutionary War are fought until the surrender of the British. France recognizes American independence. The war continues. The Peace of Paris. The British finally recognize the independence of the Americans.

1787–1791
George Washington presides at the Constitutional Conventions in Philadelphia. The American Constitution is adopted a year later, taking effect on March 4, 1789; the Bill of Rights issued in December 1791.

1793
The cotton gin, invented by Ely Witney, revolutionizes cotton farming and revives southern slavery.

1807
Robert Fulton sails on the "Clermont", the first steamboat, 150 miles from New York to Albany in 32 hours.

1808–1860
A further quarter of a million slaves are brought in, although their importation is outlawed.

1819
The steamship "Savannah" crosses the Atlantic in 29 days.

1825
Warfare with France, Tripoli, Britain and the Indians; the Louisiana purchase; Spain cedes Florida; completion of the Erie Canal opens up the interior.

1844
Samuel Morse sends a message from Washington to Baltimore over the first telegraph line.

1846
US declares war on Mexico after border clashes.

1848
Mexico renounces claims to Utah, Nevada, New Mexico, Arizona, Texas, California and a part of Colorado; Elias Howe invents the sewing machine; gold discovered in California.

1852
Harriet Beecher Stowe publishes ''Uncle Tom's Cabin''.

1861
The Civil War begins after seven southern States proclaim the Confederate States of America and fire on Union forces.

1865
Confederate troops surrender after four years of bitter fighting; President Abraham Lincoln assassinated.

1866
Alaska purchased from Russia for 7.2 million dollars.

1869
Transcontinental railroad is completed.

1875
Congress passes the Civil Rights Act, giving equal rights to blacks, nine years after the founding of the Ku Klux Klan in the South to terrorize blacks from voting; Mark Twain's ''Tom Sawyer'' published.

1878
The era of the commercial telephone begins.

1893–1897
Economic depression.

Above:
   Trinity Church Tower in New York, by Harry Fenn.

Left:
   Old houses in Savannah, by Granville Perkins.

277

A Glimpse of Fifth Avenue, New York, by Harry Fenn.

1894
First public screening of Thomas Edison's motion pictures.

1903
First automobile trip across the USA; first successful flight, for a distance of 120 feet and duration of 12 seconds.

1911
First transcontinental flight, with many stops.

1917–1918
The submarine war launched by Germany to break the British blockade precipitates US entry into the First World War; a million American soldiers pour into Europe.

1920
First regular licensed radio broadcast.

1923
First 'talking' picture screened in New York.

1924
George Gershwin writes "Rhapsody in Blue".

1927
Charles A. Lindberg makes the first non-stop flight across the Atlantic in 33 1/2 hours.

1929
Stock market crash inaugurates the Depression.

1931
Opening of the Empire State Building revives optimism.

1935
George Gershwin writes "Porgy and Bess".

1936
"Gone with the Wind" by Margaret Mitchell published.

1939
Albert Einstein advises President Franklin D. Roosevelt of the possibility of the atomic bomb; the USA remains neutral in the European war.

1941–1945
President Roosevelt inscribes the four freedoms on the US banner: freedom of speech and religion, freedom from want and fear. Japan attacks Pearl Harbor on December 7, 1941; USA declares war on Japan, Germany and Italy. After Germany's surrender, the dropping of two atomic bombs forces Japan to capitulate.

1947
US assists Europe under the Marshal Plan.

1948
British and US planes enlisted to break the blockade of West Berlin.

1949–1953
Korean War.

1954
First voyage of the atomic-powered submarine "Nautilus". Fierce clashes over racial segregation in public schools.

Since 1955
Twenty years of military involvement in Vietnam begins with US agreement to train South Vietnamese army. The space race starts; black Americans revolt against discrimination; Soviet Premier Khrushchev visits America; abortive US attempt to overthrow Fidel Castro by the Bay of Pigs expedition; President John F. Kennedy, Rev. Martin Luther King and Robert Kennedy are assassinated; Neil Armstrong is the first man to walk on the Moon; President Richard Nixon undertakes peace mission to China; Nixon is compelled to resign over the Watergate scandal; US troops withdraw and communist forces take over South Vietnam.

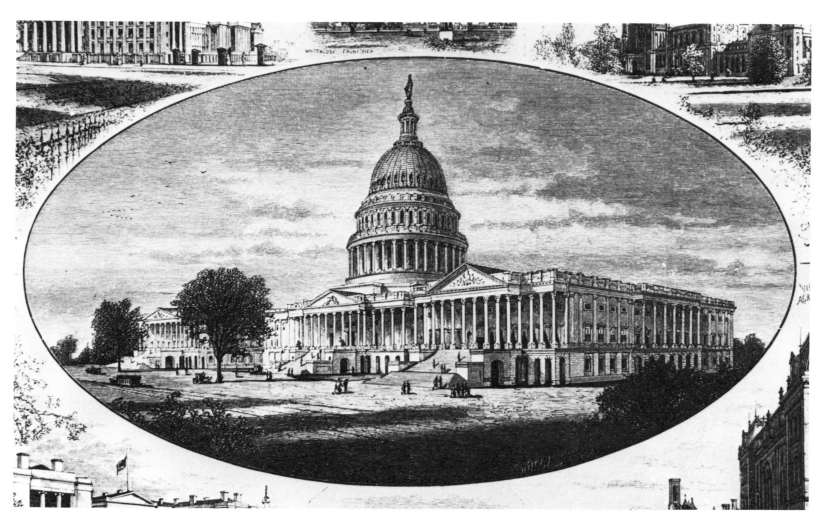

The Capitol, Western Terrace, by
W. L. Sheppard.

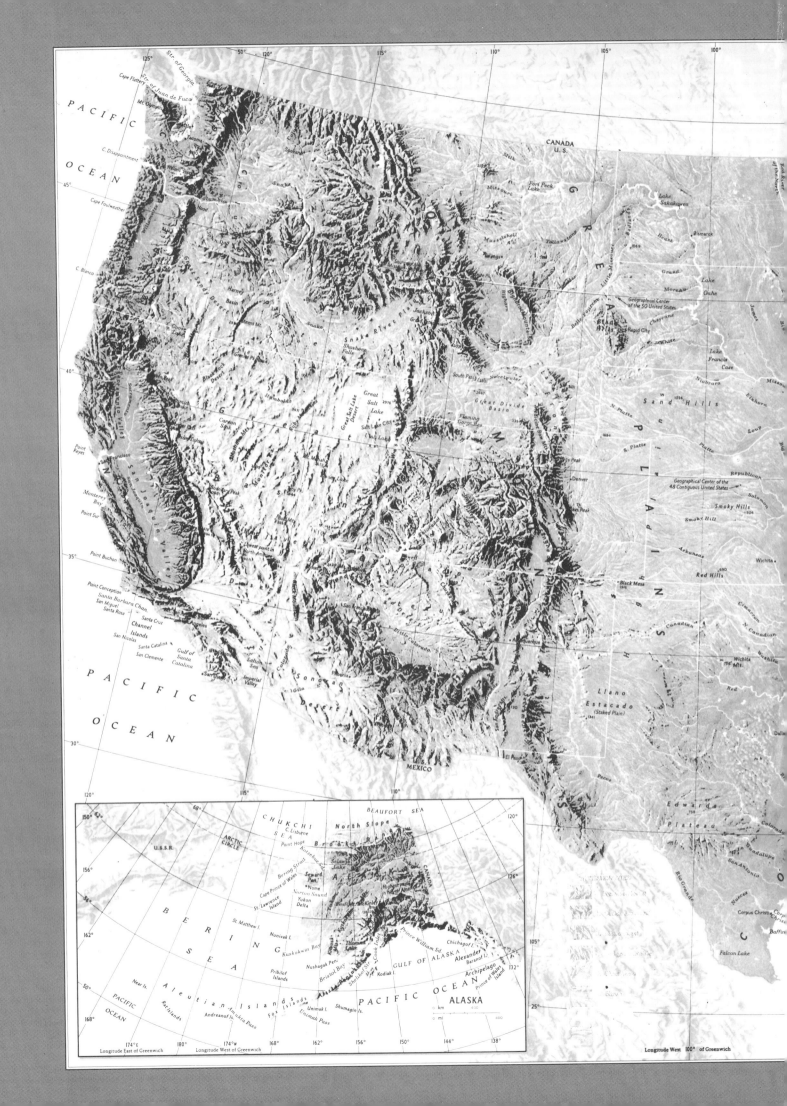